Tony Levene, former Investment Editor of *T* is now a freelance writer. He has also worked *Review*, Thomson Regional Newspapers as deputy City Editor and *Financial Weekly* as News Editor.

Tony Levene's other books include *Planning for Retirement.*

THE
SHARES
GAME

How to Buy and Sell Stocks and Shares

Tony Levene

Pan Original
Pan Books London and Sydney

First published 1987 by Pan Books Ltd,
Cavaye Place, London SW10 9PG
9 8 7 6 5 4 3 2
© Tony Levene 1987
ISBN 0 330 29923 9
Photoset by Rowland Phototypesetting Ltd,
Bury St Edmunds, Suffolk
Printed by Richard Clay Ltd,
Bungay, Suffolk

Contents

I should like to thank all the Shares Game players who helped and
guided me in the writing of this book. I have acknowledged some
in the text but I am indebted to all whether I have incorporated
their observations or not.

   But most of all, I should like to thank my son Oliver, born just a
few days before Big Bang, for allowing me to sleep at night, my
daughter Zoë for telling me to get on with my work whenever my
spirit weakened and to my wife Claudia for her support during a
difficult time and for the index.

Introduction

Britain has caught the share-buying bug. Something like eight million adults – and a substantial number of children – now own a share in at least one company. And that figure is rising every day.

In 1983, there were less than three million shareholders and their number was falling, a phenomenon helped by tax rules which encouraged the moderately well off to sell their shares to an insurance company to avoid paying Capital Transfer Tax. This tax was abolished in the March 1986 budget.

The government and the City trumpet these figures. They are very flattering. It seems that the British people are changing from being building society depositors to being share-owners.

But other statistics are given less publicity. These show the proportion of shares in UK companies held by the public.

At the end of 1986, the value of all the shares quoted on the London stockmarket was £300bn. Of that total, just a quarter was held by individual investors. The rest was held by large financial institutions holding shares on our behalf in pension funds, insurance companies and investment and unit trusts. Despite the growth in the number of individual shareholders since 1983, the gap between the proportion of shares bought and held directly and those bought and held on our behalf remains unchanged.

The Shares Game is about closing that gap. It explains how to move from being a shareholder in one or two companies to becoming a fully fledged investor. For most new converts to the Shares Game have not yet ventured outside the major privatisations, such as British Telecom or British Gas, or their employer's shares which they may have obtained through an incentive scheme. The Shares

Game will also give you insights into what the institutions do with your money.

Buying shares appears to be complicated. There is a City mystique. Phrases such as 'modern portfolio theory', 'reverse yield gaps', 'pre-emption rights', 'Bulldog bonds' and 'price earnings ratios' are used. There are alphas and betas, gammas and deltas bandied about. There are economic indicators. There are point and figure charts. Every profession has its jargon. Lawyers love Latin, doctors prefer 'cardiac arrest' to 'heart attack', and no one in the digging business calls a spade a spade.

You can ignore much stockmarketese. Learning the fine points of modern portfolio theory will not make you rich. It has done little for the fortunes of its full-time proponents. Some you will need to know. You do not have to understand the finer points of football to know that the basic rule bans players from picking up the ball.

The first rules of the Shares Game state:

1 Shares go up when there are more buyers than sellers.
2 Shares go down when there are more sellers than buyers.

There is a third rule.

Whether an individual buys or sells is determined by the interplay in each investor of greed and fear. No one can predict which of these two forces will predominate.

There is one final rule. Investment is not a science, there are no set rules. It is an art and one that is open to all.

Reading a book on chess will not turn you into a grandmaster, but it will show you where the pieces go. With experience and practice you will progress.

The Shares Game has an equally modest aim. Unlike some other guides to investment on the stockmarket, it does not promise to show you how to make a killing or even that it will make you money. There are no guaranteed schemes or magic methods. You should steer clear of anyone who claims to offer such guidance. If they possessed the real secret of successful stockmarket investment, they would be putting it into operation, not writing about it.

The Shares Game stresses the element of unpredictability in the stockmarket. The current price of a share is a balance of every good and bad element that has already been published or which can be easily assumed. Share prices move when the unexpected happens –

and they often do not move in the way that past experience or the 'experts' tell you.

The Shares Game will show that you are likely to do better than many professionals by selecting shares with a pin. There is a jargon name for this as well. It is called the random walk. It is a concept that is so simple that most react with incredulity. It is a theory that professionals detest. They make their money by telling you which shares to buy and which to sell.

The first aim of the Shares Game is to help you avoid getting 'killed' or losing all your money. Its second aim is to explain the nuts and bolts of buying and selling shares. The third is to provide a strategy that is simple and inexpensive to put into action. And finally there are pointers on how investment professionals think.

As in any other game, you need just one extra ingredient. LUCK!

1. What is a share?

Just what is a share? One answer for players in the Shares Game is that it is a piece of paper bearing the name of a company and a number. The owner of the share may not know what the company does. And the company will normally neither know nor care who buys the shares. This piece of paper is known as a certificate. Its value goes up on some days and down on others. Wherever the price goes, or even if it stays the same, its relationship with other shares in the national and global stockmarket will change.

The answer is, of course, far from the textbook definition. Yet it contains a large measure of truth. Before embarking on a more formal explanation of what a share is, it is as well to state from the outset that shares need not always have a close relationship with the world of industry or commerce. Many British industrialists argue that the stockmarket with its passion for day-to-day performance may hold back the growth of industry and commerce – the very opposite effect to the one claimed by the Stock Exchange. They point to the great postwar growth periods of Japan and West Germany which were financed through long-term money from the banks. They also calculate that less than 10% of the new money needed in industry and commerce comes from the stockmarket. The reply is that the stockmarket acts as a barometer of the economy and of each company whose shares are quoted on it. A stockmarket somewhere will always provide finance for ventures ranging from the absurd to the absolutely safe – at a price.

The debate over what the function of the stockmarket should be is never likely to be resolved. It is one that those in the Shares Game can ignore. Investing in shares, or equities as they are often called, has nothing to do with patriotism. Some of the most successful investors over the past decade have put all their money into Japan or West Germany. And harsh as it may sound, it has nothing to do with creating employment or helping industry to modernise. It is all to do with making the best use of your savings.

There is little connection between the short-term performance of a company and its short-term performance in the stockmarket. British Telecom shares doubled within a very few days of their sale to the public in late 1984. A few months later, they had more than trebled in value and anyone investing £800 initially could have made a clear profit of some £1,600. Yet the phones did not double or treble in efficiency over that period. There were probably just as many wrong numbers and noisy lines. In early 1986, you could have bought a share in British Telecom for 278p. Later that year, they were worth 178p. Anyone buying at the higher figure and selling at the lower would have lost over a third of their money. Yet there was no noticeable deterioration in the service or its profitability.

What had changed in both the steep rise and the steep fall of the shares was the all-important factor – sentiment. Stockmarket sentiment is the amalgam of all the fear and greed, of all the conflicting theories and thoughts on the future direction of a share price. In the British Telecom case, this had little to do with the quality of telephones. The price of the shares were governed by a host of other factors which make up sentiment. These ranged from the decision of the Japanese government to sell its own telephone system to the Japanese public through fears of a future UK government committed to renationalisation or deprivatisation to, perhaps, a hangover suffered one morning by the manager of a pension fund which had invested heavily in the shares.

Shares did not start out with such a loose relationship with the business world. Perhaps the first examples of sharing were the co-operative hunting efforts of our earliest ancestors. They realised pooling resources – running ability, weapons and snares – would result in more food to eat. Obviously, no one was going to throw their lot in with their neighbours unless the meat was shared out.

Nearer our own time, merchants realised that there was a greater degree of safety from attack if they combined their ships into fleets or their pack animals into caravans. If each of ten merchants contributed one ship to the fleet and nine made it safely back to port with their cargoes of silk, then each one would have a one-tenth share of the proceeds of the trip irrespective of whose ship was actually sunk or captured by pirates. If one merchant had two ships, then he would have a two-tenths share.

The big breakthrough came one day when one of the merchants said he needed cash urgently. The castle overlooking the sea he had always wanted had just come on the market. That might have been an excuse. Perhaps he had heard that the entire fleet had been lost but he would obviously have kept this quiet otherwise everyone would know that his share and all the others were worthless. Today, he might be found guilty of insider dealing.

Whatever the reason, he sold his share to someone who was not one of the other shipowners at a mutually agreeable price before the fleet returned home. Trading in shares was invented.

This new purchaser's relationship to the fleet was different to the others, who had contributed a ship and who expected to sit back and wait to see how much the cargoes fetched. They were primary investors. They had contributed their ships, their money and their trading skills in the silk business to set the venture up.

Our new shareholder was not a shipowner. He may have had no knowledge of the silk trade. But he was taking a view on the future. He had to hope that the ships were bringing back silks and not sand, that the colour of the silks would find a ready market with the beautiful people of that time and that the route taken by the ships would avoid storms, rocks and pirates.

Before the fleet arrived, our new shareholder became worried that the ships were sailing into a pirates' trap. But three other people in the waterside bar he frequented thought otherwise. They believed the ships were taking a route through calm crime-free waters. Moreover, they believed that the cargo was even more valuable than was first thought as the silks were dyed in the designer colours that would be shown – so they had been told by a contact in the rag trade – at next week's fashion show. They were taking a view on the future. It was a different one but a stockmarket can only function if there is a variety of views.

The share was divided into three smaller shares and sold at a profit. If the latest shareholders had been misinformed on the fashion show, they risked having to sell their shares for less than they paid for them once the truth became known. While one shareholder feared pirates and sold, other shareholders were bullish (stockmarketese for optimistic and the opposite to bearish) about the contents of the cargo. They bought.

All this time, the fleet was sailing around the world, buying silk,

fighting off pirates and avoiding rocks and storms. The constant sale
and resale of the shares had no effect on the ships. The financing of
the voyage had been completed before the fleet set sail. The officers
and crew had no idea who was buying and who was selling. And the
reasons for and against investment in the fleet that were put forward
in its home port may or may not have had much relationship with
what was actually happening to the ships.

Eventually, the fleet came home intact, the silks were just the
right colour and the venture made a huge profit. Each share or
divided share was cashed in for its due portion of the earnings. Had
the fleet come back in tatters having lost all the silk, then the
shareholders at that time would have received very little or perhaps
nothing. But whether the end result was good or bad, it could have
no effect on those who had sold their shares previously.

The only difference between that and modern company shares is
that today companies continue in business until they are either
bought lock stock and barrel by another company or they go bust.
The buying and selling of shares on the basis of a mixture of genuine
information, half-understood facts, rumours and sometimes downright lies continues.

The waterside drinking holes and merchants' coffee houses have
given way to stock exchanges and computerised electronic dealing
rooms. The human element with all its strengths and weaknesses
remains unchanged.

Any benefits you get from investment in a share are worked out
according to how many you own. What you paid for them does not
matter . If there is a dividend of 5p per share or if there is a takeover
bid at £5, that is what you get whether you paid £1, £5 or £10 for the
share.

No one can prevent you becoming a shareholder in a public
company – identified by the letters PLC (public limited company).
You can be as rude as you like to the company directors and even if
you were to assault them and get sent to prison as a result, your
shares could not be taken away from you. You can vote to get rid of
directors that you do not like. You can call company meetings. You
can vote on company issues by post. You have to be sent an annual
report and certain other documents. You can send someone to a
meeting in your place who would then be able to voice an opinion
and vote. You can do lots of things because you own the company.

Or rather, you and many others own the company. Some of your co-shareowners may own a far bigger slice than you. Major share-holders are likely to be institutional investors – a convenient phrase for banks, charities, insurance companies, investment trusts, unit trusts, investment management companies and pension funds. Financial institutions own the great majority of shares. In 1983, they owned 78% of all shares according to Phillips & Drew, the stock-brokers. Twenty years previously, they owned 42% of the total. The recent huge increase in the number of individual shareholders has barely dented the 1983 figure.

The more shares you have, the greater your power. Your rights as an individual shareholder have to be seen in that context. Small shareholders do not change the direction of companies. Large shareholders rarely do so either. They dislike washing dirty linen in public. No matter how well founded it may be, a public row risks sending the share price into a nosedive. They may occasionally exert behind the scenes pressure for change. They find it easier to set up a united front against an errant company because investing institu-tions know each other and can liaise through various committees. But as a rule, they take the easy way out pleading that ownership has to be kept separate from management. Investing institutions in West Germany and Japan take a different view.

All the employee shareholders of British Telecom amount to no more than around one per cent of the total shareholding. Even if they could all be persuaded to vote on one issue in one direction, no one would notice. British Telecom has over one and a half million small shareholders. Taken collectively, they have less votes than a comparative handful of institutions.

Shareholders have the right to attend annual meetings. Very few do so. At some meetings there are no shareholders present other than the directors. A few companies which are not too happy to have any public presence or comment hold their meetings between Christmas and New Year in an obscure location starting at an early hour in the morning. A few companies do attract shareholders to their meetings. Some come in gratitude to praise the board, no matter what it might have done short of cutting the dividend (which is the only unforgivable sin). A few ask inane questions about some obscure part of the company's business. And there are the campaig-ners who buy one share as their admission ticket and then use the company meeting as a well-publicised soapbox for their views. This last group makes the best use of annual meetings. Their protests rarely find sympathy with the majority of small shareholders who tend to be conservative, elderly and in favour of hanging, drawing and quartering for stealing a bag of sweets. Nevertheless, they can always count on good press coverage. They know that they will provide the only element that will wake whatever poor journalist has been sent to cover the meeting.

Some years ago, the Imperial Group, now part of the Hanson Trust, was under fire for its production of tobacco, fizzy beer, battery hens and one or two other things as well. To keep the meeting orderly, the group's public relations department arranged that each protest group should have a set time and would be able to deliver a statement to the press.

A few companies reward shareholders who attend with a free meal or a bag of the company's products. Some do not even offer a glass of sherry, pleading poverty even if they have laid on a lavish meal for their more important shareholders afterwards. With companies such as British Gas, TSB and British Telecom having several million shareholders, it would be physically impossible for even a small fraction of the shareholders to attend a meeting.

You have many legal rights as a shareholder. Only two really count – your right to buy and your right to sell.

2. **Risk**

Shares are a risky investment. Buying a share may mean that you will make a profit. There can be no certainty no matter how attractive the purchase looks or is made to look. Shares carry just one guarantee, however. The most that you can lose is the price you paid for the shares together with the cost of buying them. If a company goes bust you cannot be asked to put your hand into your bank account and fork out more cash, no matter how much the company owes. A number of companies do go bust each year.

Reputation alone does not save a company. Some very well known names in British industry have ended up either in intensive care or in the knacker's yard – Laker Airways, Rolls-Royce (aero engines), Alfred Herbert (machine toolmaker), Fodens (trucks), British Leyland, Dunlop as well as virtually the entire British toy industry. Some have recovered, although with no benefit to the original shareholders.

Because share buying involves a risk as well as a reward – and the relationship between these two factors will be considered later – no one should buy shares until they are satisfied of their own personal fitness to buy them. You would not play tennis if your fingers were broken and your legs were in bandages. You would not play Scrabble if your ability to spell was poor.

The Shares Game is no different. One of the cardinal rules that anyone selling shares or other investments to the public has to obey under the new investor protection legislation is the commandment to 'Know your client'. Professional investment advisers have to be aware of the wealth and the financial needs of their clients. If those selling investments have to weigh up the client's circumstances, then it is even more vital for you to take your own circumstances into consideration. The rule is 'know yourself'. In practice, this means two things – knowing your own temperament and knowing your own financial circumstances.

Will you sleep well at night knowing that even the most successful shares have their off days? Shares in Jaguar, the luxury car group, were sold to the public at 165p each in July 1984. The shares soon doubled to 330p, then went down to under 250p before climbing again. In 1986, the value of one Jaguar share was anything between a low point of 335p and a high point of 585p. Moves of 20p in a day – either up or down – often happen. Could you take these ups and downs with equanimity or would these movements cause you worry and depression?

Do you find it hard to make up your mind? Are you the sort of person that buys three items of clothing and then returns two or even all three to the shop because your views on style change once you get home? If that is you, then shares are not for you. You can seek all sorts of advice and ask your broker every half hour about the state of the stockmarket but once you have purchased or sold shares, then you have committed yourself. There is no cooling off period when you are given the luxury of changing your mind. Most brokers and other dealers involved in the stockmarket tape record all phone calls. They should tell you about this but as many do not, you must assume that your conversation is being taped.

If you make a mistake, you can reverse the transaction but there will be costs involved. There will of course be times when shares will be bought and sold profitably within a short time. As a rule, however, look on a share purchase as a longer-term investment. The costs in buying and selling soon become prohibitive otherwise.

Potential investors need to consider how much risk they can take, tied up with whether they can afford the worst case – losing all their share investment – without it having a disastrous effect on their lifestyle. So before you invest money in a share, check that you can afford it. Ensure that you have covered the essentials of personal financial planning. A mortage and adequate life assurance cover, to protect your family should you die, come before share deals. Put to one side an amount to cover large items of expenditure that might occur over the next two years such as holidays, furniture, carpets, domestic appliances, car repairs, repairs to your home and anything else that might go wrong. On top of all that, allow yourself an additional slice of safety to protect you from unforeseen events.

This cash should be kept in a building society where it can be withdrawn instantly. Raising money by selling shares to cover either regular expenditure or emergencies could mean that you are forced to sell at an inopportune moment. It also means that you could wait anything up to three weeks for your money. This could be too long in an emergency.

The alternative to selling would be to get a loan. Borrowing cash like this can be very expensive. Remember that very few shares grow in value as fast as interest on an unsecured overdraft or on a loan from a credit card company.

The self-employed and anyone not in a company pension scheme should also ensure that they have made sufficient provision for their retirement before investing in shares. You can claim tax relief on any money going into a pension scheme within certain limits (17½% of earnings from most sources other than investments for those born in 1933 or later with a slightly higher level for those born earlier). And once invested, these pension contributions suffer no tax whatsoever.

The great bulk of pension fund contributions end up in shares somewhere in the world. Add the two layers of tax freedom together and anyone buying shares out of taxed income and paying both income tax and capital gains tax would have to be very lucky indeed to beat a pension fund. Anyone in a company scheme but who has fallen behind for one reason or another should consult their company pension scheme administrator for details of additional voluntary contributions. Putting your money into a pension certainly lacks the glamour of buying and selling shares on the stock exchange. You will not be able to tell your friends of your investment skills. You will, however, have added a vital piece to the jigsaw of your personal financial planning.

As a result of soul-searching and working out your personal financial position, you may consider that you do not wish to invest in shares. Fine. If you read the rest of this book, you will get an idea of how a fascinating part of the financial make-up of the country works. And you have not wasted the money spent on buying this book. It costs less than the commission a stockbroker would charge on even the smallest share deal.

If you have decided that you can live happily with the undeniable risks of investing in shares, the next stage of 'know yourself' is to discover what you want from shares.

Some investors do it for the thrill. They compare it with having

£10 to win on a horse running in the 2.30 except that with most shares, your money keeps on running much longer – backwards as well as forwards. These investors are happier seeing £500 going up to £1,000 over three months than to have £5,000 grow by 20% to £6,000 over the same period. The percentage gain is all that matters. They may move in and out of the stockmarket or even a particular share with amazing rapidity. They will be active investors ready to back rumours and half-formed views. They note with approval that most newspapers place their racing pages next to their City pages.

Others take a longer-term view, investing part of their money in shares as part of a careful strategy which takes their past, present and future tax positions into account. Most investors are some-where between the two extremes. Positioning yourself somewhere between conservative tortoise and radical hare will help you work out your future course if you decide to take your share purchasing beyond £200 in TSB or £150 in British Gas. Knowing how much risk you are prepared to accept will help you decide on the sort of shares you should purchase.

There is a risk involved in shares although it is less than in commodity trading where it is easy to lose all your money in five minutes and then face a bill from a commodity broker for more money. There are risks in stuffing your money under the mattress where it could be consumed by fire or eaten up by inflation and bedbugs. And there are risks involved in putting money in a supposedly safe haven such as a building society. The risk in this case is that you will miss out on the gains to be had elsewhere.

But while there are risks, the stock exchange is not the casino its detractors accuse it of being despite the habit of calling the highest quality shares 'blue chips' after the most valuable counters on a roulette game. Unlike a gaming house, it is possible for all the players in the Shares Game to show gains. Since the end of 1974, share prices in the UK have risen tenfold. A roulette wheel merely distributes the chips from one player to another with the casino operator taking a percentage. Shares Game players cannot cash in all their chips at one time, however. If everyone was selling and no one was buying, there would cease to be a market. It can happen in some shares.

Such unanimity over the stockmarket as a whole just does not happen. Even in the great Wall Street crash of October 1929, there was constant buying and selling. The market did not hit rock bottom until the summer of 1932 and in the intervening years, the US

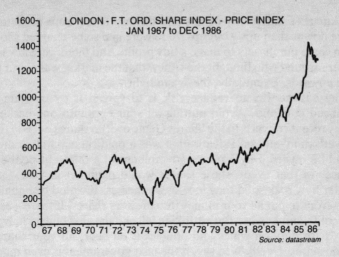

LONDON - F.T. ORD. SHARE INDEX - PRICE INDEX
JAN 1967 to DEC 1986

Source: datastream

F.T. 30 INDEX ADJUSTED FOR INFLATION £100 INVESTED
JAN 1967 to DEC 1986

Source: datastream

Shares have been a good investment. The twenty year graph for the two decades since 1967 shows a steady long term upward movement. Even the great bear market crash from 1972 to 1974 is no more than a short term blip in a long term move. Adjusting the index for inflation shows a less optimistic picture but from 1975 onwards, shares on average have outpaced inflation. The inflation adjusted chart ignores the dividend income from the shares. Reinvesting that into shares would produce a steeper upward graph that would have beaten inflation over all the years except for the early to mid seventies when inflation was at its highest. Governments stocks, building society accounts and gold bullion have not beaten inflation.

stockmarket saw plenty of ups and downs. There were of course more downs than ups – but ups there were and some enabled short term share purchasers to make a tidy profit. And there were always buyers around who thought they knew that the market was about to turn upwards. Eventually, they were right.

The easiest way to reduce risk is to spread it by creating a balanced portfolio. Avoid putting all your eggs into one basket. Many recent converts to the Shares Game own no shares outside the 'privatisation' stocks. Privatisation was a political act and as such could be reversed by a future government of a different political stance. In that event, these shares would plummet in value, no matter how rock solid they look as businesses. It would be equally dangerous to put all your money into brewery shares. If there was a wet cold summer when beer drinking fell or if the next budget halves the excise duty on wines and doubles it on beer, all your shares would suffer. Needless to say, if the next government is even more firmly wedded to privatisation or if the weather and tax changes gave beer drinking a boost, the opposite would happen and all the shares in the group – the stockmarket calls them sectors – would go up.

Knowing yourself will determine what degree of risk you can live with. Over long periods, investors who take higher risks – investing in small companies for instance – are rewarded providing they have avoided the 'all your eggs in one basket approach'. Over short periods, this strategy can cause big ups and downs in your wealth.

The risks inherent in buying shares cannot be avoided. You – and you alone – bear the ultimate responsibility if your shares turn sour. There is another risk, however. And that is fraud or incompetence by a share dealer.

You probably bought your first shares by filling in a coupon in a newspaper and pinning a cheque – and your hopes – to it. That is fine if you simply buy new issues. At sometime, however, you will want to sell these shares or you will want to buy shares that have already been issued – one of the 7,000 or so stocks and shares dealt on the London stockmarket. You have encountered the 'secondary' or 'after' market.

Buying a share as a secondary investor or selling ones you already own needs the services of a stockbroker or a licensed dealer in securities. You will have to entrust this person with your money if you are buying or with your shares if you are selling. Very occasionally, things go wrong. Cheques for shares sold mysteriously get

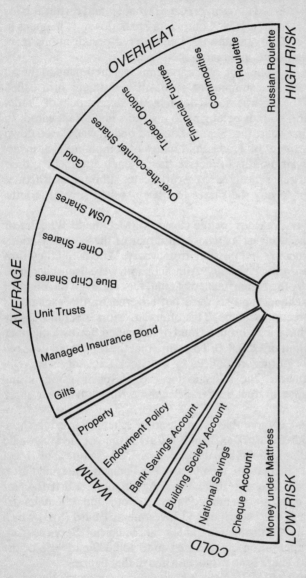

OVERHEAT

HIGH RISK

Russian Roulette
Roulette
Commodities
Financial Futures
Traded Options
Over-the-counter Shares
Gold

USM Shares
Other Shares
Blue Chip Shares
Unit Trusts
Managed Insurance Bond
Gilts

AVERAGE

Property
Endowment Policy
Bank Savings Account

WARM

Building Society Account
National Savings
Cheque Account
Money under Mattress

COLD

LOW RISK

How much risk are you prepared to take? The greater the risk, the greater the reward provided you do not put all your eggs into one basket and are prepared to be patient. Once the risk spectrum gets to the overheat level, you risk losing all your money before time has a chance to work for you. Traded options could lose you all your money in a month or two, commodities in a few days, roulette in a few hours. Russian roulette could affect your health more than your wealth in a few seconds.

Choosing blue chip shares, the cornerstone of the 'choose 'n' hold' strategy gives medium risk, but a better reward than other investments including property whose value has to be assessed after the payment of rates and maintenance charges.

lost in the post or even more mysteriously are thrown in the local canal by a disgruntled messenger. Contract notes and certificates for shares purchased go astray. Computers break down. It happens in the best ordered organisations. Well-ordered organisations react quickly to complaints and rectify their errors.

Companies in trouble or where someone has their hand in the till do not. In the late summer of 1986, an investment firm called McDonald Wheeler was closed down by the Department of Trade. Several million pounds belonging to investors had disappeared. In November that year, the 'Share Shop' in London was closed down by the Department of Trade amid scores of complaints that investors had to wait months to receive their money after selling their shares or had never received share certificates although the cheques they had sent to buy the shares had been cashed several months before.

Whatever the reasons for the closure of McDonald Wheeler or the Share Shop, investors who used either of these organisations suffered financially and possibly from worry. Who could they turn to for compensation? Nobody. Although both were licensed to deal in securities by the Department of Trade, they were not members of the stock exchange and so were not covered by the exchange's investor protection scheme. This offers investors a refund of any money they have lost through fraud or incompetence by a member firm up to a limit of £250,000. To ensure that the fund is not used too often, member firms are policed by the Stock Exchange's surveillance department. The scheme does not cover investors losing money because a stockbroker gave the wrong advice on share buying.

There is no comparable compensation scheme covering share dealers outside the stock exchange and at the time of the McDonald Wheeler and the Share Shop difficulties, there was none at all. Most of these share dealers are members of the Financial Intermediaries Managers and Brokers Regulatory Association (FIMBRA for short). This now offers a limited investor protection scheme under the umbrella of the Securities and Investments Board (SIB) which oversees investor protection under the Financial Services Act. There is compensation on all losses up to £30,000 and 90% of the next £20,000. There is no protection above that figure.

Dealing with a FIMBRA share dealer means foregoing the better compensation fund and the stricter policing that stock exchange members undergo. The second cost is that your name and probably your telephone number go down on their client lists. You will then be pestered at home by high pressure salespersons to buy shares that neither you nor any self-respecting stockbroker has heard of. You will be invited and cajoled into reinvesting the profits you made by selling a blue chip such as British Telecom or TSB into companies selling second-hand fruit machines in South America or which have miracle cures for unmentionable diseases or which claim to have found a way of growing grapes in Greenland. As the section on over the counter shares suggests, the best thing is to put the phone down. There is nothing illegal in what they do. The problem is that many of these dealers do not adequately explain the higher risks involved in the shares they sell in the over the counter market. Again, once you have agreed to buy or sell through such organisations, then you must complete your side of the bargain even if you realise as soon as you put the phone down that you have made a costly mistake. Your phone conversation will have been tape recorded. A failure to come up with a cheque will almost certainly result in court action.

These harsh comments by no means apply to all FIMBRA members, most of whom are content to sell insurance bonds and unit trusts. But they do apply to some of the companies which tout their dealing services in newspaper advertisements.

3. Finding out what is going on

The City appears to devote its energies to share certificates or their electronic equivalent. It does not. It revolves around information. Information whether it is correct, half correct, a quarter correct or just a damn good story, is one of the essential lubricants of the stockmarket. The second is interpretation – the ability to decide just what percentage of a piece of stock market information is correct and what emphasis to give it in the context of other available information. Knowing where to find information is just the first half of the game but in the Shares Game as in any other, a good first half is usually an essential prerequisite for victory.

You need information whether you adopt the fundamental analysis approach or the choose and hold strategy. But if you are prepared to take the random walk theory to its extreme form of picking stocks with a pin or if you have full faith in technical analysis, you can ignore this chapter.

The City produces masses of information each day – both from within its own resources and from specialist providers outside. A large fund management company may receive anything up to half a hundredweight of paper on a busy day as well as a non-stop torrent of electronic information conveyed via a battery of screens. Backing all this up will be filing cabinets full of company accounts and other historical data.

All this information splits neatly into three sections. There is that relating to the past, to the present and to the future. Information purporting to predict what will happen is by far the most important. As we have seen, the role of a stockmarket is to discount the future – to attempt to forecast or guess the fortunes of a company or an economy. To do this with any degree of confidence demands background. You need to know what is happening in the present and what has happened in the past – not for its own sake but as a key to the future. Reading and interpreting old annual reports – and all annual reports are old as soon as they are published – may be interesting but unless that information can be related in some way to the future prospects of the company in question, then reading them is time wasted.

Playing the Shares Game involves knowing how the professionals play even if you do not adopt their methods. They get their information from eight main sources. Two of these sources are beyond the scope of private investors. Professional investors are often invited on organised visits to companies so that fund managers can quiz directors and senior executives in private. Sometimes they invite themselves and if the response is less than warm and welcome, they form their own conclusions. Professionals also have their own internal research capacity. This often means a large department of analysts which the private investor cannot duplicate.

There are six other sources of information; the financial press, stockbrokers' reports, city opinion, financial commentators, information released by the companies themselves and independent published sources. All these other sources of information are available to private investors at least in part. But before you try to garner in as much information as is available to fund managers controlling hundreds of millions of investments, remember that information costs money and interpreting information costs time. Just buying the main daily and Sunday newspapers that carry financial information would cost at least £600 a year. Add in a few weekly and monthly publications and a bill at your newsagents of £1,000 a year is within reach. More specialised services can cost many thousands of pounds a year. For a large fund management company or big stockbroking firm, the cost is incidental. Missing just one useful piece of information can cost tens of thousands if not more.

In September 1986, the Harris Research Centre, a market research and opinion poll organisation carried out a survey of 183 investment managers for Extel who publish a variety of financial information.

The survey found that research and information gathering is steadily growing in importance with many fund managers saying that they spend more time on these tasks than a year previously. But while most of the survey concerned itself with computerisation of information sources – a subject beyond the spending power of most private investors – the attitude of City professionals to major sources of information and how they trust those sources has lessons for all players in the Shares Game.

The first question in the Extel City Survey on Research and Information Gathering was:

When making investment or business decisions, which sources do you get most of your information from?

Financial Press	40%
City Opinion generally	4%
Brokers' reports	77%
Internal research	16%
Financial Commentators	1%
Information from companies	39%
Independent published sources	37%
Company visits	4%
Other	7%
Don't know	1%

(The figures add up to more than 100% as fund managers were allowed to give more than one answer. Most gave either two or three sources for most of their information)

Contrast that with the following question

Of those sources, which would you trust most?

Financial Press	28%
City Opinion	4%
Brokers' reports	50%
Internal research	51%
Financial Commentators	5%
Information from companies	61%
Independent published sources	26%
Company visits	2%
Other	1%
Don't know	1%

In general, the professionals look first at brokers' reports and at the financial press. These are sources of immediate ideas and it could be dangerous to ignore them. But, as the survey showed, professional players do not trust them to the same degree. They have more than a shrewd idea of how stockbrokers and their analysts work. They have an equally clear idea of how stories arise in newspapers. They trust their own internal resources and they also trust information released by the companies themselves. Fund managers neither use nor trust company visits to any degree.

Information that is untrustworthy can cost you a lot of money. But if you know that information is inaccurate, don't expect your superior knowledge to be reflected in the share price as long as the false information is believed by others. Eventually, you may be proved right – by which time, the stockmarket might be assessing the shares on a new base. A number of mistakes need to be made before the City stops believing in a certain source. One error is not enough. In the meantime, it can be expensive to hold out against mass opinion. For a basic rule of the Shares Game states that the direction of a share price is decided by the comparative weights of money brought into action by buyers and sellers. Whichever is the heavier decides if a share goes up or down. There are no absolute rights or wrongs. The purveyor of the false information might have a very good past record or may be looking at the share from a different direction. The City is forgiving of mistakes – until they happen too often. And fund managers find safety in sheltering behind the orthodox.

Financial press

This covers a wide range of publications ranging from the *Financial Times* through the City pages of quality daily and Sunday newspapers such as the *Daily Telegraph*, *Guardian* and *Observer* as well as more popular newspapers such as *Today* and the *Daily Mail*, weekly publications such as *Investors Chronicle*, the *Economist* and *Financial Weekly* to monthly investor magazines including *What Investment* and *Money Observer*. Many newspapers published outside London both in the morning and afternoon have space devoted to City affairs. It is a growing market with new titles appearing all the time. In addition, there are television programmes such as the Money Programme.

Coverage of the Shares Game by the financial press fits neatly into two categories. There are facts – share prices and company profit figures – and there is interpretation, forecasting and share tipping. Professionals do not need the facts as they have their own electronic screen services. They look for interpretation but long experience has taught them to treat it very cautiously.

It is a question of what you pay for is what you get. Fork out forty pence a day for the *Financial Times* and you get the most complete list of share prices in the country outside the extremely expensive *Stock Exchange Official List*. It is not a complete list but it includes most companies quoted on the Unlisted Securities Market and many of those on the new Third Market. Companies have to pay the *FT* (as that pink newspaper is universally known in the City) £875 per year for each class of share that is to be quoted. Some other newspapers have similar arrangements. There is no obligation on a company to have a share price in the *FT* or any other newspaper for that matter. The *FT* quotes share prices for some of the biggest foreign companies on its main prices page. It also covers, although in less detail, the main companies on a variety of foreign stock exchanges on other pages. However, virtually all companies quoted on the over the counter markets made by sharedealers are not listed either in the *FT* or elsewhere. Some of the dealers take paid advertising space to publicise their prices in the *Sunday Telegraph* and the London *Evening Standard*.

For the price of a quality paper, you get around half the number of share prices that the *FT* contains with very few overseas companies although the quality of detail remains. More popular papers give a short résumé of share prices with little additional detail other than the amount by which the share has gone up or down since the previous day. This format is of little help to players in the Shares Game.

Finding shares can be difficult in some newspapers. To ease comparison between shares in companies involved in broadly similar activities, most newspapers divide shares up into categories instead of simply running an alphabetical list. Some of these section headings are confusing. Drapery and Stores is used in more than one newspaper. Drapery conjures up the image of a tiny shop selling pretty ribbons and laces. It would appear to cover interests in textiles although the rag trade would perhaps be a better name as another group of companies appear under the heading 'Textiles'. Department stores are listed under Drapery and Stores as are do-it-yourself supermarkets but not builders' merchants and newsagents and bookshops. Food supermarkets are found under 'Food and Catering'.

The *Guardian* insists on differentiating between electricals and electronics and has a separate column for Unlisted Securities Market stocks. The *FT* has Newspapers and Publishers, lists television companies under Leisure and puts advertising agencies in a separate category where they are lumped together with packaging makers and printers. The *Independent* has a Media category which lists newspapers, publishers, television companies and advertising agencies. Headings such as Industrials (Miscellaneous) and Trusts, Finance and Land can be even more mystifying.

New issues are normally contained in a section of their own. How long a new issue remains new depends on the newspaper.

An alphabetical list would make more sense but the present system is not just rooted in history, it can also provide clues to a company's future course if that company undergoes a change of category. News of a move from boring Industrials to exciting Electronics or from breweries to leisure can often put several pence on a share price because the company is seen to be switching from an area of dull performance to one more in tune with the glamour sector of the day. No company would ever choose to move to a duller sector.

You cannot take the printed share price as any more than a rough guide although typographical errors are exceptionally rare as most newspaper prices lists are printed directly from a computer linked to a stock exchange prices service. The prices in a morning newspaper are those ruling at the close of business the previous day. They are likely to change as soon as the stockmarket opens in the morning. More importantly, the prices given are the middle market prices halfway between the bid price you get if you are selling and the higher offer price you pay if you are buying. The marketmaker's spread is ignored – as are all dealing charges. Different newspapers may quote different prices. Not all newspapers take their prices from the same source or at the same time each day. In a rarely traded stock, price differences can occur because one information system relies on the last actual deal while another relies on the last quote regardless of whether business was done at that price or not.

If a broker or any other advice-giver tells you that a share is at its high or low point for the year in the *Financial Times*, ask how long that year is. Assuming it is early spring, the answer may be four or five months and not twelve months. The 'year' may start on 1 January. If this information is being given as a preamble to a recommendation to buy or sell a share, you will need a clearer picture. You will need to find out the figures for the previous twelve months. But you should not ignore this information. As long as the great majority of other players accept it as significant, then it is significant. Information in the market can only be judged by the standards of the stockmarket.

Share prices are usually expressed in pence although gilts are quoted in pounds and shares over £10 are quoted in pounds and fractions of a pound. The fractions are sixteenths or thirty-secondths – equal to a 6p or 3p unit respectively. American, Australian, Irish, European and South African stocks are generally quoted in sterling but not always. Check. Some European shares are very 'heavy' – buying one share costs hundreds or even thousands of pounds. Shares in Allianz, the West German insurance group, stand at around £800. The plus or minus figure here would be in whole pounds.

The next figure is the change on the day and will vary from newspaper to newspaper for the same reason as there might be variations in the price of the share itself. This far, the more upmarket newspapers keep to a common formula except that on Saturdays, the *Guardian* replaces the high and low figure with the market capitalisation of the company – a figure in millions or billions which gives the value of all the shares in issue of a particular company and on Mondays, the *Financial Times* gives details of the dates of dividend payments. It also shows companies that have not paid dividends for some time. A company that last paid a dividend in October 1977 would be shown as '10'77' while one that paid out on July 1st would be '1,7'.

Most lists show the yield, expressed as a percentage without any deduction for tax. They may also give the cover – how many times that yield can be paid out of earnings – and the price earnings ratio, which divides the price of the share by the earnings per share. In addition, the *Financial Times* gives the net dividend per share, which enables you to work out exactly how much your next dividend cheque will be worth.

For many shares, either the dividend or the price earnings ratio or both are absent – to be replaced by a dash. This can occur if the share is in a sector such as insurance where price earnings ratios are regarded as inappropriate. It may occur if a company is too new to have a record – in its first six months as a public company, for instance. But the most usual reason for a line of dashes is that the company has failed to make any money and therefore has no earnings to compare against its price. It will probably not have paid a dividend either.

If you are looking for undervalued shares that might come back into vogue, then selecting shares with a row of dashes is the first step to finding a bargain. Needless to say, others will be adopting the same strategy – some more speculative share traders around the City say they refuse to buy a share unless it has a row of dashes. It is a high risk strategy.

Newspapers also print a mass of blobs, daggers, asterisks and other special symbols conveying information such as a share going ex-dividend. Different newspapers use different symbols and the *Financial Times* has the most hieroglyphics.

The other function of daily newspapers is to print company results and offer comment. The comment – whether in the section marked 'comment' after a company result in the *Financial Times* or in a column such as Lex in the *Financial Times* or Questor in the *Daily Telegraph* – will tend to be a journalist's interpretation of a conversation with one of the stockbroking analysts covering that company. Journalists do not often have the time to ask more than one analyst for an opinion but if they do, the view of the analyst who provides the better 'story' – perhaps one who has a different view to everyone else or who says something controversial – will tend to be used. Analysts provide these comments on an 'off the record' basis so their names rarely appear. The Lex column in the *Financial Times* is read far more assiduously by the professionals than any other. It is required reading because everyone else will be reading it.

The *Financial Times* gives results and some comment for virtually all companies but much of the comment outside the Lex column is written by junior journalists. Other newspapers tend to cover big companies and either ignore small companies or reduce their figures to a few lines unless the company is especially newsworthy.

The City coverage in Sunday newspapers is quite different. They have no fixed agenda of daily news such as company results, share prices and economic announcements clattering over their tape machines or appearing on their screens. It is rare for anything to happen on a Saturday and most of the Sunday newspapers' coverage of business and the City is written earlier in the week.

This means they have the freedom to escape the fixed agenda of market reports and company news in the daily newspapers and can write stories at length. One example is the investigations into financial malpractices that the *Observer* does well. It also means that the journalists can be short of inspiration. The public relations machine knows this and many stories in Sunday newspapers are fed by friendly PR agents. Journalists do not wish to offend their friends in the PR world and so many of these stories lack objectivity. Stories of companies coming to the stockmarket for the first time are usually written without criticism.

Some Sunday newspapers also specialise in running many stories on takeover rumours – often on the thinnest of evidence. Using this scattergun approach, some are bound to happen and the paper then boasts of its success. Much the same scattergun approach is seen in the share tipping columns where again journalists rely on publicity machines and on friendly stockbrokers. Few bother to ask stock-brokers if they have a position in the stock. These columns are often put together in record time on a Friday evening. At at least one Sunday paper, there is a queue of PR personnel lining up to give the City staff titbits about their clients – or nasty stories about their clients' rivals. Some of these papers print the PR story without changing, checking or challenging a word.

There is no evidence that any of these columns perform any better than a stab with a pin. But if you are tempted, check to see if the market follows the advice on Monday morning. This will show whether the professional players believe there is any value in the column. Work out how much a week's worth of share tips has fared after one day, one week and one month and compare that against the stockmarket index. Try and discover if the market makers push up the price the next morning to trap the unwary. Repeat this for several weeks. If you are impressed by the overall standard, make sure that any average of shares is not distorted by one or two very good performers which stand out among a heap of dross. You cannot afford the scattergun approach because you cannot afford to buy every share that is tipped.

It is not uncommon for a share to go up on a Friday because, so the City gossip machine says, it is to be tipped in a Sunday paper. It has not been unknown for unscrupulous dealers to invent such a story to help rid themselves of a line of stock or for the occasional journalist with a position in the share to spread such a story. These columns have all the drawbacks of tipsheets. They at least have the merit of costing nothing.

The most useful weekly magazine is the *Investors Chronicle*. It has a good statistical coverage and writes about most shares that have announced results. It is the cheapest and easiest way to build up a filing system covering company results. Its views on shares tend to be conservative. It provides a good sounding board to bounce ideas against even if you do not accept them. *Financial Weekly* covers companies at lesser depth but devotes space to giving short résumés of stockbrokers' circulars. Monthly magazines such as *What Investment* suffer from the length of time between the writing of an article and its appearance but it can give a good general background. *Money Observer*, also a monthly and connected to the *Observer* newspaper has a useful analysis of percentage changes in share prices over one month, six months and one year. It also offers good coverage of investment and unit trusts. They all offer advice of what to do with your investment money and recommend shares. Although their record is no worse than anyone else's, their tips do not generally move the stockmarket.

Television currently offers little for players in the Shares Game unless you have Teletext, the Ceefax and Oracle services which are transmitted daily at no charge other than the need to have a more expensive television set. Both Ceefax and Oracle give share prices regularly updated through the day but for space reasons, both services are confined to the shares with the biggest market capitalisations. The maximum number of gilts and shares covered on the present system is around 200. There is also regular City news including company results and advice on unit trusts.

Of all the sources of published information, stockbrokers' circulars are the most forward looking. Much of the material which appears elsewhere owes a large debt to the circulars and their analyst authors. It is rarely acknowledged. Circulars cover a wide range of companies. Others concentrate on the state of the economy, the gilts market, stockmarkets and economies outside the United Kingdom or specialised investment areas such as options and futures.

They are part of the great City paperchase. Each year, forests are cut down to provide the paper and each day huge wastepaper bins full of circulars leave the offices of fund managers for pulping and conversion into cardboard. Despite their frequent use as a primary source of information – they suffer from drawbacks. Too many are produced and few are of good quality. They are also expensive. The output of a medium-sized research department costs £200 a year just to print and post. You would need to buy and sell shares worth over £15,000 just to cover those two costs alone. And you must add to that the six-figure salaries that some analysts get and the cost of the research itself. That cost factor means that while fund managers, newspapers and others involved on the inside of the Shares Game receive more than they could possibly read, small investors have to beg to get on the mailing list.

Big Bang will eventually change this. With the end of fixed commissions, stockbrokers are examining each facet of their service and many are moving towards 'unbundling' – making a separate charge for each part of their service so that you only pay for what you get. Some stockbrokers have already made tentative advances towards turning their research departments into separate profit centres by the sale of research material. Providing that you are willing to pay, you could buy circulars. But what material has so far been sold is expensive. Unbundling will also sort out the good from the bad. No fund manager is going to pay for poor research.

There is little variety in the physical appearance of circulars. The main factor is the recommendation on what to do. It will say buy, hold or sell although some brokers give further graduations of the 'strong buy' or 'weak hold' variety. A few will use stockmarketese such as 'reduce weighting'. Very few circulars ever say 'sell'. Stockbrokers do not like telling clients to sell. They fear the proceeds will be reinvested elsewhere. They are happier in advising clients to 'switch' from one stock to another with a similar business profile but allegedly with better prospects. This does not leave their clients with the problem of what to do – a difficulty that many small investors feel when they sell a share for the first time. The broker also picks up two sets of commission.

Straight sell advice is also problematic because most analysts like to keep good relations with the companies they watch. Much of the information they relay to their clients comes from the companies themselves – often by way of unofficial meetings and hints. Many brokers submit their work to the company in question for checking – especially if it is a major study. Therefore it is doubly difficult to advise a 'sell'. Phrases such as 'reduce sector weighting' or 'weak hold' are often coded ways of saying 'sell'.

Many readers stop at the recommendation. Further on, there is a summary of the main points followed by forecasts of profits, dividends and earnings per share for the current company years and sometimes the following year as well. The profits forecast is a key figure. The main body of the circular may range from a short amplification of the main points to a detailed account of the company's activities. A long circular may be used to impress the company under consideration if the broker is touting for that company's corporate advice business. Fund managers may find it harder to throw away a 200 page effort than one consisting of just two sides.

Circulars are backed up by phone calls to fund managers either from the analyst in person or the institutional sales staff whose job is to ensure that any buy order in that share comes to the stockbroker producing the research. The analyst's function is to produce business. Choose and hold or random walk have no place in their vocabulary.

The all important factor on a circular is the name of the broking firm producing it. Each year, Extel, a major publisher of financial information organises a poll of leading fund managers to see who the best research analysts are. Despite a thirteen-year existence, it is hardly surprising that its methods and end results are challenged by those who do not end up in star positions. But outside the disappointed, most professional Shares Game players would be hard put to disagree with its most general findings. In 1986, the top ten brokers for overall research were:

1. James Capel
2. Phillips & Drew
3. Scrimgeour Vickers
4. Wood Mackenzie
5. Hoare Govett
6. Barclays de Zoete Wedd
7. Warburg Securities
8. Greenwell Montagu
9. County Securities
10. Alexanders, Laing & Cruickshank

This is a list which has remained largely unchanged over the past few years. The top three have been unchanged for the past three years. Out of over two hundred broking firms in the country, only twenty-four appear at all in the Extel survey and only three of those firms – Gilbert Eliott, Henderson Crosthwaite and Vivian Gray – are outside the big league. In some ways the Extel survey is self feeding – in common with much else in the City. Fund managers and journalists use the survey to decide who they will contact in any market sector where they do not have prior contacts. A good analyst at a firm outside the list knows that one way of progressing in a career is to aim at big firms which tend to be good at marketing themselves and their analysts. Big firms also offer better back-up facilities and higher salaries.

The difficulty is that to even get a sniff of the original material from one of the best research houses you would need to be a client of one of these firms. Few in the top ten list will accept clients with less than £50,000 while survey leader James Capel demands a portfolio of at least £75,000 for discretionary management and no less than £150,000 for an advisory service.

This does not mean that you are left out in the cold. Most research adds little to the total sum of useful human knowledge. When a major circular is produced, most stockbrokers get to hear about it quickly. No stockbroker sends circulars to rival firms but fund managers will happily tell their friends in the broking fraternity about the more interesting contents of their morning's post. Many brokers send all their research material to the press which often reprints key details such as a change in recommendation or a new profits forecast. And there is *Earnings Guide*, a monthly publication taken by most stockbrokers which carries details of most profit estimates.

If there is anything that is 'price sensitive' in a forthcoming circular, it would be normal practice for the analyst or the sales staff to give selected clients unofficial extracts of what is in the circular ahead of its publication. The idea of the leak to the large institutional holder is to help the market on its way to the desired goal. When the circular comes out, other players in the Shares Game can see that the share price is already on the move. The normal herd or bandwagon effect takes over and the share moves further in the desired direction. It does not always work so smoothly. The market may pick up a confused or totally erroneous rumour. It may also decide that the broker in question has a poor track record and do exactly the opposite. A third possibility is that the market will move in the wrong way between rumour and publication.

The small investor has an advantage in receiving the contents of a circular at second hand. A journalist or stockbroker can act as a filter, cutting out the obvious rubbish and putting the research in a global context. You can make up your own mind free of any phone calls from over eager sales staff.

The Extel survey shows that the average analyst is aged 33½ years, has been an investment analyst for 7 years and covers 34 companies – an average which covers small companies specialists who may look at anything up to 200 companies in a year to those whose role is to look at very specialist areas such as tobaccos or pharmaceuticals where there may be less than half a dozen companies of any size. Analysts, who increasingly hunt in teams, tend to

spend relatively little time on shares outside the top 100. Their role
is to generate business and while a study of some small emerging
company with profits of £500,000 may be interesting and a pointer to
a star company of tomorrow, there may simply not be enough shares
around to deal in and thereby earn commission to justify the analyst
spending several weeks looking at the company.

Even the leading investment analysts are often mediocre at
understanding the sometimes seemingly irrational forces that move
markets. Many can tell you all about nuts and bolts production for
the past twenty years and a particular company's share of that
market but are as surprised as a total novice investor when the
stockmarket fails to respond as their rational research methods
would suggest. Looking at the top analysts, 79% of the fund
managers said the analysts had a very good knowledge of the areas
they researched but just 31% praised the success of their recommendations as highly.

City opinion

As a source of information and guide to the future, City opinion is
notoriously hard to pin down. For some, it will mean following the
herd – doing what everyone else does in the sure knowledge that
there is safety in numbers. For others, it is a euphemism for keeping
an ear close to the City gossip machine. For a third group, it is
simply distilling every scrap of information that can be gathered in
the hope that several heads are better than one.

City opinion is a force that cannot be ignored in the short term
when it can move markets violently. In the longer term, it seems to
have little relevance.

City opinion may also be a cover for concerted action by the
powerful. A group of powerful insurance companies sat down
together at the end of 1974 at the height of the worst bear market in
living history when City opinion was freely predicting the end of the
capitalist system as we know it, and decided to buy. A week or so
later, the market revived. At the time, before details of this meeting
were widely known, a change in City opinion was given as the
reason for this reversal.

Financial commentators

Financial commentators – independent observers of the market
scene – are more a feature of Wall Street than of the City. Certain

commentators appear to have caused Wall Street to fall or rise. Whether they do or not is as debatable as the old question of the chicken and the egg. What happens is that a commentator calls the main market moves correctly for a time. He (hardly ever she with the exception of the mysterious Aidan sisters who predict the price of gold from their hacienda in Costa Rica) tells the world or a select group of subscribers that the market is about to reverse in direction. Once this has happened twice or three times, the word gets around and all that the sage has to do is to predict and the prediction becomes self-fulfilling. This may happen once or even a few times. Joe Granville, an American tipster, telexed all his clients with a 'sell everything' message some years ago. They all sold, the market plummeted. He did it again. The New York market fell again. Then he attempted it for the third time. The market soared upwards. Granville took to forecasting earthquakes. His clients had either to buy back into the market or lose out on a long bull phase. He lost most of his clients but a few stayed, maintaining a mystical faith in their guru.

Commentators may make a virtue of consistency. Some will predict the collapse of share prices through a long bull market. Others will forecast a new revival for shares throughout a long bear market. Both are content in the sure knowledge that one day or another, they must be proven correct. Financial commentators – a term that includes some of the nation's more pretentious journalists – spend their time looking almost exclusively at the future. If any had the deep understanding of the markets they claim, they would be making money quietly not telling all who would listen.

Independent published sources

There is a great variety of independent published material to help in selecting shares. Much of it is prohibitively expensive for the small investor and is only available in major public libraries. The greater part of this material is aimed at the historical perspective. Increasingly, it is being made available in the form of on-line databases which can be accessed for a fee. This should enable these sources to be used more. Libraries no longer have to go to the expense of buying material, filing and storing it.

The two most important historical services are *McCarthy Cards* and *Extel Cards*. Neither is actually printed on card. Both services are unique. McCarthy cards reproduce all the newspaper cuttings on a given company. The service covers all British quoted companies (including the USM), a number of companies quoted on one of the various over the counter markets and a selection of large unquoted companies. Reading them can be tedious – the profits figures of a major company may be repeated five or six times over in virtually similar words. One drawback is that small items mentioning the company – normally in the context of a market report – are often ignored. Consult McCarthys if you are considering investing in a small company. Sometimes, going back some five years or so shows up interesting and subsequently hidden aspects of a company's past or that of its directors.

As McCarthys are updated rapidly, you can check whether that tip a certain newspaper gave you was original or whether it had been copied from a rival which published it the week before. McCarthys prints cuttings from all the main national and provincial daily and Sunday papers, weekly magazines such as *Investors Chronicle*, *Financial Weekly* and the *Economist* and from principal foreign newspapers. But the service does not cover tipsheets and some of the more obscure investment magazines.

An Extel card is a potted version of the report and accounts of a company over the past ten years. It details share prices, profits, sales, and taxation. It also gives recent balance sheets, the most recent chairman's statement, the company's bankers and other advisers, its registered address and phone number and the address of its registrar, which is useful if you have problems with share certificates or dividend payments. The main cards are updated annually. They are backed up by 'news cards' which are issued more frequently. News cards cover items such as interim profit reports, rights issues and changes of director.

Information released by the company

Information emanating from the company itself is the most controlled. No company is going to freely publish detrimental material about itself. But because of the laws governing company reports and stock exchange rules telling companies what they have to publish about themselves in certain circumstances such as when they are issuing new shares, in some ways it is the most complete. Every company has to publish annual accounts. Stock exchange rules demand that each quoted company publishes an interim report to cover the first half of its accounting year. The scope of this can vary from a brief statement and some very sparse figures to a publication not far from the size of the annual report. In addition, a few companies publish quarterly reports. These tend to be companies with a sizeable United States shareholding. Quarterly reports are obligatory in the United States. Regard any tardiness in publishing reports without a very good reason as worrying. One City saying that can be relied on is 'Bad figures take longer to add up than good'. These figures can sometimes take so long that the company can go bust before the directors get a chance to sign the report.

Companies often release technical details of their business to the relevant trade magazine or publish it themselves as a glossy brochure. Company newspapers can often be worthwhile sources of information with items such as changes in personnel or news of new machinery. Equally, the non-appearance of a company newspaper can often be the sign that the company has hit trouble.

All this information has to be made publicly available. Companies are not permitted to disclose details of their activities to selected shareholders which could give them an unfair advantage. As almost all information that has not been publicly released could be deemed to be price sensitive, that severely restricts the scope before an accusation of insider dealing is made. It has to be to everyone or to no one. That does not mean that every shareholder has to be sent every word uttered by the company by registered post although interim reports and full year accounts have to be sent to the shareholder's registered address. A press release to the newspapers counts as a public communication to all shareholders.

However, companies break this rule every day much as they might deny it. They give unattributable briefings to journalists, they have lunch with stockbrokers. It is barely conceivable that no price sensitive information passes between directors and brokers over the second bottle of madeira. What else are they supposed to talk about? A share price might often change after such a lunch and no one is left in any doubt that it was a result of something someone gleaned between courses. There has to be some end product other than a convivial lunch.

Companies also leak information through their public relations consultants who pass it on to friendly journalists. This rarely results in any harm but it enables companies to transgress rules on public statements. There are constraints on companies talking to the press during takeover bids. A public relations consultant, who will be sitting in on meetings between the board of the company and its bankers and other advisers, can release details where the company and its advisers cannot. If anyone complains, it can be claimed that the public relations consultant has no official role.

This leads to companies using this route to put out disinformation about their opponents.

Our random walk and choose and hold strategies imply that share tipsters are no more successful than picking shares with a pin. It is a contention that tipsters would condemn. Undoubtedly, tipsters do find winners. Some even tell you when to sell. But how do you choose a tipster? Is it worth paying anything from £50 to £500 a year to subscribe to a tipsheet newsletter? Substantial evidence from the United States says you are wasting your money. Most tipsheets adopt the scatter gun approach. They tip many shares knowing that some will hit the target. Your problem is knowing which tip to back and which to shun. There is less problem in choosing which newspaper tipster or tipsheet to follow. They are all much the same.

In 1983, the Consumers Association carried out research on the New Year tips of three Sunday newspapers, one daily, two magazines and two tipsheets over a seven-year period. It assumed you held the shares for one year and compared the average of each periodical's tips and the overall average against a basket of shares with a similar risk reward ratio. It found that most of the shares went up in price the morning after the tip was published. (The *Observer* now makes an allowance for this.) Take away the 'tipping factor' and the average of all tips actually underperformed the basket of shares by a small proportion. Using the tipster's own prices, the tipped shares slightly outperformed the basket. The best tip went up 384% in a year (assuming you could have bought at the recommended price). The worst fell by 65% – and that ignores the cost of buying and selling.

The verdict in *Which?* magazine was 'Over a year or so, tipsters in general did slightly better than we would have expected if they'd used a pin to pick similar sized companies.'

4. Portfolio

Buying shares and investing in the stockmarket sound like two ways of describing the same activity. Life is not that simple. They can be different concepts.

Forget shares for the moment and look at books. Anyone who goes into a bookshop and buys a book is a bookbuyer. Possessing one or two books does not make a library.

Shares are much the same. Thanks to the privatisation campaigns, millions of people now own shares in just one or two companies. As their confidence grows and they find out more, they may buy one or two other shares. Now they are in the first stages of investing in the stockmarket.

To play the Shares Game, you need to think in terms of investing a substantial slice of your savings after making provision for all the essentials such as a 'rainy day fund', your pension and mortgage. If that leaves you £2,000 and you put £1,000 into shares, you are investing in the stockmarket. If that leaves you £200,000 and you put £1,000 into shares, you are not. This may not necessarily be wrong. One of the rules of playing the Shares Game is to have a reserve of cash. A second rule is not to commit money to the stockmarket if you lack confidence in future trends. But this second rule implies that you have sound reasons and you have not kept your money in the bank simply out of apathy or inertia.

Investing in shares also implies a sensible strategy. You should spread your risk with a portfolio of shares. So how do you construct a portfolio? If you have enough cash available for investment, you could create a portfolio yourself or ask a stockbroker to do so for you. In either case, you will need to think in terms of at least ten shares although twenty to twenty-five should be considered the upper limit because of the time it takes to check on their performance and prospects and because academic studies in the United States have shown that spreading your risk any further achieves nothing.

You need at least £5,000 for a portfolio. It is possible to start with less, but you then run into the problem of the relatively high cost of dealing in small amounts.

If you do not have enough money available for personal portfolio building then the answer is collective investment such as a unit or investment trust. Some have a minimum investment requirement of as little as £250 and monthly savings schemes starting at between £10 and £50. These will be considered in detail in the chapter 'Leaving it all to someone else'.

Before you start portfolio building, it is back to the basic rule of 'know yourself'. You need to list your investment objectives. These can include risk free investment, saving for a specific end, investing for a regular income with an element of growth, investing for growth, speculative investment and pure gambling. The variety is infinite. You may find you have more than one objective and that they are as mutually exclusive as a pub crawl and a temperance society meeting.

The way to deal with these apparent contradictions is to follow the lead of professional fund managers and apportion your cash. If you have £10,000, you might set £1,500 aside for aggressive speculative forays with the rest reserved for more restrained investment. Large pension funds often follow this route appointing one fund manager to look after the bulk of the fund with a restrained target and a second fund manager to take on a smaller part of the fund with the order to manage the money aggressively, take greater risks and attempt to maximise the return.

If you follow this course, keep to it. If you lose all the cash you set aside for speculation, leave it at that. Take it as evidence that you are not best advised to enter into short term speculations. Very few people are. Never try to double up to recoup losses. It makes no sense at the racetrack. It makes no sense in the stockmarket. If the rest of the portfolio does well, then try again with £1,500 at a later stage. In the interim, try and work out where things went wrong.

You can, of course, split your portfolio into as many sub-sections as you wish – and devise your own. The only limitation is your financial and time resources. Spread either too thinly and your portfolio will become shapeless, expensive to manage and difficult to track.

Risk free investment

No investment is risk free. You always risk missing out elsewhere. Index-linked gilts offer the nearest solution for investors who want to sleep easy at night. They offer a guarantee that the original investment will be repaid on a set date with the capital adjusted for inflation. The yield is also inflation proofed.

The problem is that as with all government stocks, it is only possible to ignore market forces until the bond matures. You then face the need to re-invest and that means choosing whatever is on offer at that particular moment. If you have a clear investment objective, then you can organise your portfolio to some degree by choosing the date when you feel you will be able to reinvest. Index-linked stocks have varying maturity dates. The present list has stocks maturing in 1988, 1990, 1996, 2001, 2003, 2006, 2009, 2011, 2013, 2016, 2020 and 2024. A stockbroker or bank will tell you the precise date in each of these years when the index-linked stocks mature. Those that mature in the far distant future are well liked by pension fund managers who like to have a firm base on which to plan well into the next century.

Few private investors would want or need to do that. Only the nearer dates make much sense with the index-linked stock called Treasury 2% – 1996 is probably the furthest into the future that most would want to consider.

Saving for a specific end

Your investment strategy may have a specific goal such as a child's eighteenth birthday, school or college fees or a wedding. The traditional way of saving for a specific end is to entrust the money in question to an insurance company. There are a number of draw-backs with this course besides the very obvious fact that you might buy a policy with a company with a poor investment record. The difficulty with the insurance route is the costs involved with the policy and the inflexibility of many policies. If you buy an insurance policy, part of your cash will be used to pay a commission to the person who sold you the policy and part – the amount depending on such factors as your age, sex and health – will go towards paying for insurance benefits such as a lump sum on death which you may not require.

Additionally, insurance companies do not like investors cashing in early. There may be financial and taxation penalties if you need your money before the policy reaches its maturity. These can be especially serious if you cash in during the early years. You may need to do this if your goal disappears or moves.

With this sort of investment strategy, it is best to get a safe base. Start off with gilts which you buy with maturity dates close to your objective. This will give you the chance to sell into an earlier upswing while still guaranteeing an eventual fixed sum. Part of your capital should also be invested in convertible shares. This will enable you to lock into a fixed return while having the chance to take a profit by converting into equities.

Do not expect too much from such a portfolio. Set yourself a modest target so that you are not tempted to take undue risks. It helps to have a calculator or computer capable of compound interest. As a guide

Turning £1,000 into £2,000 over five years needs an annual compound return of 14.9%

Turning £1,000 into £1,500 over five years needs an annual compound return of 8.4%

Turning £1,000 into £2,000 over ten years needs an annual compound return of 7.2%

Turning £1,000 into £3,000 over ten years needs an annual compound return of 11.6%

Turning £1,000 into £5,000 over fifteen years needs an annual compound return of 11.3%

All the above calculations ignore inflation, taxation and dealing costs.

Investing for income

If you are into your seventies, the easiest way to invest your money for maximum income is to turn it all over to an insurance company and buy an annuity. This will give you a guaranteed income for the rest of your life. The only snag is that neither you nor your heirs ever see your original money again. If you are younger and need a very large rate of income, you might be persuaded to use your money to buy income producing assets such as transportation containers. If you can find a company that does not steal your money – and many high publicised companies in container leasing have done just that – you might end up making 15 to 20% on your money for between ten to fifteen years.

At the end of that period, your assets fall apart with rust. You have again sacrificed your capital for income. This is rarely wise with a tax structure which penalises income more heavily than capital gains.

Other than by sheer luck, you cannot have both high income and high capital growth. Investments are a play-off between one and the other. Any investment that promises you both is either foolhardy or fraudulent. Income also plays a big part in determining where an investment fits on the spectrum of risk and reward. A rule is that the higher the income, the lower the risk. Your balance between capital growth and income is a personal one.

Building society and bank accounts, national savings, gilts held to redemption, local authority bonds and insurance-based guaranteed income bond will all pay you a regular income but give you back no more than you paid in. You run the risk of inflation eroding your original capital. If prices fall, as they did during parts of the nineteenth century and the 1930s, you will do well.

A measure of capital growth will protect your money against the worst ravages of inflation. It will mean your accepting a lower income at least at the outset. If your immediate circumstances allow you to do that, you will have to concentrate on investments in shares. You will need to find a new statistic – the average gross dividend yield of the 700 plus companies monitored in the Financial Times-Actuaries All Share Index, known as the FTA All Share although it is far from containing all shares. In January 1987, this stood at around 4%, a little above the level a year earlier but half the peak level seen in late 1976 and early 1980.

Playing the income plus capital growth game should eventually give you more capital and more income than if you had left your money in a building society or bought gilts. Your risk will be higher, but over a long period investors are always rewarded for accepting a higher degree of risk. If you had invested £1,000 in an average building society account in March 1981, you would have received almost 50% more income than putting the same amount of money in the County Extra Income Unit Trust. Four years later, because dividends tend to rise and only fall in a crisis, the income from the County trust edged ahead of the building society. A year further on in March 1986, the income had grown to the stage where unit holders were getting 10% more than building society savers. At the same time, the original money in the building society was still worth £1,000 while the County Bank investment was now worth £2,445 after all costs. This is not an isolated example created by careful choice of fund and time period. The principle applies to a wide variety of funds over almost any medium to long term period.

Selecting an income portfolio could also mean ending up with more profit than by opting for an aggressive growth portfolio. Over recent years, professional fund managers who bought shares offering a higher than average income did better than their counterparts who invested solely for growth assuming that dividend income net of basic rate tax was reinvested in shares.

To find income shares, scan a list of shares and mark all those offering more than the average plus a certain figure which only you can determine. One common yardstick is the average plus a quarter. With the average at 4%, you would then ignore any share yielding less than 5%. If you decide on a ultra-high income strategy, you might select only those yielding the average plus a half, in this case 6%. You will find few shares worth buying yielding much more than the average plus a half unless you are prepared to take a far higher risk. You will see some stocks in the share listings that offer more than double the average which appear to come from perfectly good concerns. These are likely to be from companies which issue fixed interest stocks of varying types such as debentures, loans, preference shares and convertibles. One or more of these words will be included in the title, which will also contain a percentage figure and a date – Tesco 9% Convertible Loan 2002-07. These stocks can be complicated. Study the rules and the dates on which you may have to make a decision on converting into ordinary shares or other action before purchasing. A stockbroker's help is advisable.

An ultra-high income portfolio would typically contain some gilts or fixed interest stocks from companies. Owners of these stocks have precedence over ordinary shareholders if a company goes bust and so they are less risky than very high yielding ordinary shares. Shares with an average yield are among the least risky in the stockmarket. They are prevented from falling too far by the prospect of regular dividend payments and might always go up if new management moves in to put life into a sleepy company or if there is a takeover bid. Ordinary shares with very high yields can be dangerous. The company may have previously announced that it was cutting its dividend or the City might think that a cut is in the offing. Some companies pay out very high dividends while they are winding down a dying business. The main skill in choosing income stocks is in rejecting those shares that fulfil the income criterion yet are potential disasters. If you buy a share for its income-producing qualities, always ask why that share is offering the yield it does. If the answers do not satisfy you move on. There is plenty of choice in the Shares Game.

5. Gilts

Take a look at the page in your newspaper that gives information on the prices of shares. Depending on your choice of newspaper, there will be anything between a few hundred and several thousand shares listed.

Government stocks are usually the first to be listed. They are also known as British Funds or gilt-edged or 'gilts'. The gilt is a reference to the one time practice of printing the certificates on paper which had a band of gold colour around the edge. The gold or gilt colour was presumably put there to emphasise that these stocks were as good as gold. This helped Victorian investors exchange their gold sovereigns for these government promises. But as we shall see later, that promise of a gold-bottomed investment has proved to be hollow in the years since the Second World War.

Gilts are not the lifetime investment they once were. Nevertheless they represent a major slice of stockmarket activity and have a place in a well-managed portfolio. Gilts have one huge advantage over shares for the newcomer to the stockmarket. They are safer than equities because the government promises to repay them at a certain value on a fixed date in the future. This 'future' may be anything from a few days to thirty years ahead. And in the meantime, the government will pay out a fixed dividend to holders on two and occasionally four set dates in each year. No government has ever failed to do this – although in the early thirties, one government did manage to persuade holders to accept a lower rate of dividend by appealing to their patriotism.

No government would attempt to do that now. Gilts are loans to the British government to help finance the public sector borrowing requirement (PSBR). This is the gap between what the government spends and what it takes in in the way of taxes. But as nowadays gilts are held by very powerful investors all over the world, any move to cut the rate of interest without compensation would provoke a major crisis of confidence. Besides, the market has become more sophisticated in the last fifty years and there are far more subtle ways of achieving the same end which do not affect the rights of existing holders.

When the government issues a gilt-edged stock, everything is known about the stock itself. If you buy it on the day it is issued and hold it until it is repaid (technically called the date of redemption), you will receive a regular unchanging income known as the yield. Many purchasers of gilts do just that. Whatever may occur in the world economy, the regular income and the eventual repayment are secure. This can be comforting, especially in periods when equity investment looks shaky.

But between the date of issue and the date of redemption, a lot can happen. The stockmarket price of a gilt mirrors the national economy. The gilts market is sensitive to changes in interest rates, the value of sterling, the rate of inflation and other factors which come in and out of fashion such as the various methods of measuring money supply. When the price rises, holders have the choice of sitting back and doing nothing or selling at a profit. If they do nothing, they continue to get an unchanged dividend stream which may be difficult to replace. Rising gilt prices mean falling interest rates, so if you sell and reinvest the original sum, you will receive less income. You have to choose between a capital gain or lower income. When gilt prices fall, interest rates rise. It is best to sit out a fall in gilts. Selling at a loss will not produce any more income – you will need to add fresh cash to achieve that. Eventually, you will get repaid at £100 for each £100 nominal.

Gilt-edged stocks were once issued in much the same way as other shares. The Bank of England would issue a short prospectus setting out the terms and the price of the issue. Investors would apply, be allocated stock and dealings would start a few days later. This all stopped in 1979 after an incident which has ever since been entered into the City legends as the Battle of Watling Street.

Watling Street is the address of the Bank of England new issues department. Messengers and personal applicants take their forms and cheques for new issues to the third floor. The lift is small and the staircase is narrow. Back in 1979, the government issued a stock at a fixed price. But in the few days between the issue and the closing date for applications, the price of gilts soared. Investors saw that the new issue was underpriced. Applying and selling as soon as dealings started (stagging) would guarantee huge profits. The rush to get applications in ended with investors and messengers fighting their way up the stairs. The police had to be called to restore order among investors who confused the Shares Game with one of American Football.

Since then, gilts have been issued by the tender method. Instead of setting a fixed price, the government sets a minimum price that it is willing to accept. If you think that the issue will be so much in demand that it is worth paying more, you tender at a higher price. The Bank of England then decides on a 'striking price'. If the issue is not popular, this will be the same as the minimum price. But if there is a great demand, the striking price will be set higher than the minimum. In this event, investors who tender at the minimum or at any amount lower than the striking price have their applications refused. All other investors receive all they want. No investor has to pay more than the striking price – even if they tendered at a higher rate. Since tendering became the normal method of selling gilts, most issues have been sold at the minimum price. That is the price the government wants. The tender mechanism protects it from a sudden change in sentiment on the stockmarket – and from recurring riots.

Gilts have three components to their title. The first is the name – usually Treasury or Exchequer although there are still a few others such as Consols, War Loan and Conversion. These names mean nothing although War Loan still has an emotive value to older investors. The next and the first crucial part of the title is a percentage, known as the coupon which indicates the dividend yield. The final figure is a date – or sometimes two dates – showing the year of redemption. A stockbroker will tell you the exact day in the year.

Where two dates are given, the government has the choice of any time between the two dates. In normal conditions, the government tries to hold on to the money as long as possible. Stockbrokers assume that the final date is the one to base their sums upon. However, if interest rates suddenly fell to the 2% seen in the 1930s, it could be in the government's interest to pay the loan back as early as possible and raise a fresh loan on terms that suit it better. So far, this has not happened. Much the same applies to a select group of gilts known as undated, a confusing title as some carry dates – Conversion 3½% 1961 or After or Treasury 3% 1966 or After. It is the 'After' that counts. These stocks would only be repaid if the cost of the running yield became expensive. It may happen one day. But no one in the gilts market would bet on it. In the meantime, these undated stocks go up and down with interest rates and seem set to pay out the same dividends every year as they have for decades.

Gilts are always priced in pounds and the quoted figure will buy you £100 nominal of stock. If a gilt is priced at £90, investing £900 will buy £1,000 nominal of stock, investing £9,000 will buy you £10,000 of stock. The figure that appears on your certificate is the nominal value of the stock and is identical to the amount that you receive if you hold it to redemption. It does not matter what happens to the market price, the nominal amount remains the same. If you sell before the date of redemption, then the buyer will still get the same amount of nominal stock irrespective of the price paid.

The nominal value is also used to calculate the dividend yield. If a stock carries a coupon of 10%, you will get £10 (before tax) in income each year for every £100 nominal you own of that particular stock. It does not matter whether you paid £50 or £200 for the stock, you receive the same income in pounds although the effective yield will depend on how much you paid. If you paid £50, your gross yield is 20%, if you paid £100 it is 10% and if you paid £200, it would be 5%. This simple-to-calculate figure – multiply the coupon by 100 and divide it by the price you paid for the gilt – is known as the running yield and is calculated in exactly the same way as the dividend yield on a share.

Life now gets more complicated. The second component of a gilt is the number of days, months or years to redemption. If you bought the gilt at £80 and held it to redemption, you would have a profit of £20. If you bought it at £100, you would make neither a profit nor a loss while if you bought it at £120, you would make a loss of £20. Stockbrokers with powerful computer programs can calculate the effect that this profit or loss makes to the running yield. It is a difficult sum to do on the back of an envelope but many newspapers print it. As a simple example – a gilt with a coupon of 10% is priced at £95 exactly one year before redemption. Ignoring tax, the return to redemption is £5 capital gain (the stock will be repaid at £100) plus £10 dividend giving a total of £15. Expressing that as a percentage of the purchase price gives a yield to redemption of 15.79%. The yield to redemption tends to iron out the differences between various gilts.

It is easy to see why anyone should buy a gilt under its par £100. There is a guaranteed tax-free profit at the end assuming you do not have a chance to sell beforehand. But why should anyone buy a stock over £100 in the sure knowledge of a loss? The answer is you should not but professional fund managers do. A few will buy an over par stock in the hopes that it will go up even further and the fund can make a short term profit. This can be a dangerous course. If you get it wrong, then you must make a loss unless another opportunity presents itself. And as each day goes by, that opportunity becomes less likely. For the nearer a stock gets to its redemption date, the closer it will get to £100. Pension and other tax-free funds which can ignore all tax considerations can buy gilts over £100. As they are the only significant buyers, they can purchase these stocks at 'bargain' prices.

The first lesson of gilts is always to buy under par. The second is to look at the coupon. A few are much lower than the majority. These are known as 'low coupon gilts'. Examples would be Treasury 3% 1991 or Exchequer 3% Gas 1990–95. They are the government's gift to higher rate taxpayers. They give a comparative low income on which tax has to be paid but as they are issued substantially under par, anyone who holds them to redemption can pick up a tidy tax-free capital gain. Add the capital gain and the income together produces the yield to redemption, a figure which tends to be lower than other gilts as the government believes that if it is helping higher rate taxpayers to pay less tax, it should keep a bit of the saving back for itself.

The third is to look at the date – assuming there is one. Gilts are divided into 'shorts' (less than five years to redemption), mediums (five to fifteen years) and longs (more than fifteen years). 'Shorts' – or short dated gilts to be more formal – offer investors the least risk. They are near to their redemption date so that investors know they will get their nominal value soon. Longs are the most risky – the market prefers the term 'volatile'. With anything up to 30 years before they are repaid, there is a lot of scope for things to go right or wrong. Mediums attract neither the investor looking for a secure return nor the investor prepared to speculate nor the pension fund looking for a steady source of income well into the next century. Being out of favour and caught somewhere in the middle means that their yield to redemption tends to be higher and their effective price lower.

You can plot yields on graph paper. The short dated ones start low and move up until somewhere among the middle or long dated stocks there is a peak. After that, the yield curve starts to move down. This is entirely normal and there would be worries if it did not. Exactly where the peak or hump appears means a lot to professionals. The gilts market is subject to an amazing amount of number crunching. As professional investors can deal in millions very easily paying no commission by going direct to a marketmaker, the tiniest fraction of a pound on a price is significant. Big brokers have whole teams feeding facts and figures into computers looking for anomalies they can exploit. You cannot do this.

There is another form of gilt for which all the rules about par values have to be torn up. These are index-linked gilts – government stocks which guarantee to link both the dividend and the eventual redemption value to the monthly retail prices index, the most widely accepted measure of inflation. The dividend and the redemption value is tied to a set formula which is based on the RPI eight months previously. On top of the inflation proofing, there is a guaranteed extra so that your money earns a few percentage points above inflation. It is the equivalent of earning that amount in a world without inflation.

Inflation proofing sounds attractive. Gilts had been particularly hard hit by the huge jumps in prices in the seventies. Unlike shares, where prices could eventually adjust to the lower purchasing power of the pound, gilts were fixed in the maximum return they could eventually offer. Anyone who had invested £100 in War Loan at the end of the Second World War had stock forty years later which was worth around a third of that on paper. Add in the effects of inflation and that stock would buy goods worth just 3% of the original investment.

The only problem was that the introduction of index-linked gilts in 1981 coincided with the fall in worldwide inflation. Other gilts – known as 'conventional' issues – have outperformed the index-linked variety.

However, these stocks are closely monitored and there is a spate of buying on any sign that inflation is going up again. No one can be certain of the future progress of inflation. With one inflation-linked stock offering protection up to the year 2024, they represent the most solid investment you can buy. It does not sound very exciting but putting part of your money into these stocks will always allow you to sleep at night. Most of these stocks are purchased by pension funds which need to plan a long way ahead. They are comforted by the fact that even if inflation goes back to an average 10% over the next thirty years or so, their money is totally protected – and they get a real return of around 3.5% on top. Nothing else can offer that security.

You can buy gilts at your local post office, where many of the more significant stocks are available through the National Savings Stock Register. The advantages are ease of purchase, low commission rates and the payment of all dividends without any deduction for tax. You have to declare the dividend and pay tax on it later, but in the meantime, you can enjoy the money.

The disadvantage is that you do not know exactly what price you are paying. The price you pay is the one in force when the brokers acting for National Savings go into the market. That will be some time after you have passed your order over the counter of your local post office. The price could change significantly in that time. You cannot buy more than £5,000 nominal of any one stock on any one day. Your choice is also limited to the list, although this is updated from time to time.

6. Taking a random walk – and some other ways of picking shares for growth

Most players in the Shares Game want their capital to grow. They want their spare cash to mount up faster than a building society account. Over any twenty-year period since the end of the Second World War, equities have done just that. And with the exception of the great bear market of 1972–74, the same is true over five-year periods. Building society accounts only come into their own over short periods – and that is what they were designed for.

There are plenty of clues to guide you if you wish to invest in gilts or in income-oriented shares. But no newspaper list prints potential capital growth winners in bold type. So, faced with thousands of equities, just where do you start? How do you select shares to buy? There are hundreds of theories and systems to help you. There are scores of newsletters, tipsheets, newspaper columnists and even astrologers and oracles. They all claim to have the Midas touch that will turn your modest savings into riches beyond your dreams.

It is all very reassuring. Sadly, it is all rubbish. There are no magic methods to stockmarket success. The theories are often mutually exclusive. If one is right, the other must be wrong. At one time or another, tipsters and theory mongers will get it right and boast loudly about it. At other times, they are terribly wrong. Some will stay silent. Others will proclaim that they are right but that their followers should have more patience. In the meantime, they prescribe a double dose of what they were tipping.

Some of the 'systems' have entered folklore. There are those who believe that aggressive entrepreneurs looking for their next take-over victim study Extel cards which give ten-year company records. But they start at the end of the alphabet just to fool everyone. So you buy shares in companies whose name starts with a 'Z'. Another suggests that you buy during Royal Ascot. The idea is that the rich have to sell shares that week to pay for their gambling debts, offering others the chance to pick up stock cheaply.

Those ideas have some rationale. Others are more exotic. There are tipsters whose moves in and out of stockmarkets are determined by sunspot cycles and lunar eclipses. And there is a theory that the future course of stockmarkets is determined by the hemlines of skirts. The higher the hemline, the higher the market although there would appear to be an upper limit somewhere. It appeared to work in the late 1960s when the miniskirt preceded a raging bull market and the ankle length maxiskirt which followed as a reaction signalled a bear market of frightening depths.

If it makes you happy to follow a tipster, a theory or folklore, fine. Over a short period, you may do well. Over the long term, you will do no better than average, but you will have to pay for the advice you get. And don't expect the proponent of any theory or system to tell you when their game is up. A rule of the Shares Game is the market soon picks up on tips and theories and adjusts prices to compensate. If the idea works, its effect is lost as everyone does it. History shows that tipsheets and theories are more likely to enrich their authors and publishers than their readers.

Leaving sunspots and share tipsters aside, there are three methods of selecting shares to buy and sell. Two are conventional and are used by professional fund managers. The third can be used by you but as it is so simple, fund managers could not use it as they would be unable to justify their fees. You do not need to know how to read company balance sheets. It takes accountants several years of study and then any two accountants will dispute every line of a company's report and accounts. You do not need to understand Elliot Waves, Coppock Indicators or Modern Portfolio Theory. Remember how you manage your shares depends on you, your own personality, your own needs and the amount of time and energy you have available. Professional Shares Game players have to look over their shoulder at their paymasters. Your only responsibility is to yourself and your loved ones. Whether you take a wild punt or rely on a system based on the 250 day moving averages of share prices is up to you.

The two conventional methods are fundamental analysis and technical analysis. Thousands of volumes have been written about them. The simple method is the random walk. At its most basic, it suggests picking stocks with a pin. It has attracted academic attention in the United States, but is virtually ignored elsewhere. It is a theory with great attraction for the small investor but none for the professional which is why it has only ever achieved any prominence in the United States with its preponderance of private shareholders.

The random walk theory suggests that if you buy a portfolio and hold it for a long time, you will do better than most professionals who constantly buy and sell. They could never justify their fees if they adopted a strategy based on passive buying and holding. If you take the random walk, you will be outpaced by a minority of professional fund managers and by a few gifted or lucky private investors. If you can be sure that you can choose those fund managers or that you are gifted or lucky, you can skip the next section.

The random walk is a theory which frightens many investors in this age of instant communications, computer aided research and volatile stockmarkets. 'How can sitting back and doing nothing be better than active management' they argue. 'If I had bought ABC Consolidated Metals at 5p last year and sold them at £5 this year, I would have made a profit of 100 times.' But did they? Backjobbing – the stockmarket equivalent of the anglers' one that got away – passes the time in City bars but serves no purpose. For every correct decision made in the stockmarket, there has to be a wrong one. Investors must have sold shares in ABC Consolidated at around 5p and someone must have bought at £5 – perhaps on the day before the shares were suspended for ever because all the directors went to prison. And who boasts about buying XYZ International Freight at 500p before their fall to 5p?

At each move in the Shares Game there is conflicting advice from the outside world. Inside each investor there is the psychological struggle between fear and greed. You may call the right move five times in a row. That is no guarantee that you will call the sixth and subsequent move correctly. Think of what happens when you toss a coin.

You may pride yourself on your economic knowledge, your market insight and your fleetness of foot. But look at the study of Guinness in 1986. Would you have been ready for the fall in the December of that year when the Department of Trade and Industry called for an inspection? No one was. And no one on the outside can tell when a company will run into such a traumatic event or when a share that you have ignored will receive a generous takeover bid.

This is not an isolated example. Who five, ten or twenty years ago would have forecast that the Allied-Lyons would have been on the wrong end of an unwelcome bid from an Australian company or that a small photographic retailer called Dixons would end up bidding for Woolworths. In early 1983, the newspapers and tipsheets were falling over themselves to recommend shares in Mettoy. It made the Dragon computer. The shares shot up like a rocket. They then came down like the stick. The company went into receivership and the Dragon computer followed it into oblivion. No one backed Amstrad, which three years later was riding on the crest of a wave. And who would have forecast the 1973 oil price rise or its crash in late 1985 and all the effects that had on the stockmarkets of the world? The list is endless. Don't forget that fund managers pride themselves on their economic knowledge, market insight and fleetness of foot.

Over a long period, the best that anyone with a portfolio can hope for is to do a little better than the average shown by an accepted index. The only way to beat that is to buy one or two shares and be lucky. Putting all your investment eggs into one basket also means you could lose it all. Most professional fund managers do worse than the average. In fact they are bound to. A stockmarket index is calculated from a number of share prices. These prices are determined by the opposing forces of buyers and sellers. As most share trading is carried out by professionals, it follows that they determine the price of each share in the index. This might lead you to think that around half the fund managers should do better than the index and half do worse. That ought to be true but for an enormous factor which all indexes ignore. Professional management and dealing in shares are expensive.

Buying and selling a share adds up to around 5% of the value of the stock. Small investors can often pay more. Getting in and out of some of the obscure stocks recommended in tipsheets can add up to 40% of the purchase price. To move in and out of a share costs two sets of commission, stamp duty and the spread between bid and offer prices. But let's err on the conservative side and call it 5%. If you followed an active sharedealing programme and sold all the shares in your portfolio each year and replaced them by new ones, you would have to outperform the index by a large degree just to maintain an average position. If you turned over your portfolio twice every year, you would need to work even harder. If you made the right decisions at each turn, then the dealing charges will be worthwhile. But can you be sure that you will make the right decision? Full-time professional investors with massive resources get it right on less than half their decisions.

The following table shows what happens to £100 (after initial dealing charges) constantly invested at an assumed market average of 12% compound growth over four years and then sold compared to the same sum invested achieving the same rate of growth where the owner decides to change the portfolio once every year at a cost of 5% of the fund.

	Unchanged portfolio	active portfolio
0.	£100	£100
1.	112	112
2.	125.4	119.2
3.	140.4	126.8
4.	157.3	134.9

The effect is less noticeable if share prices gain more although a 12% rate of growth is better than the average performance of United Kingdom shares over the past 20 years. It implies that share prices double every six years. But if growth is slower or if the market is actually falling, the effect on your wealth of regular dealing is more marked. It is harder to beat a falling market than a rising one. The biggest percentage gains in rising or bull markets come from shares outside the main stocks that make up the index. In falling or bear markets, the reverse is true. The shares of big companies, underpinned by dividend income, hold up better. This has strategy implications if you are caught in a bear market. You cannot trade yourself out of difficulty. That is a sure course to double your trouble. If you do not need immediate access to the cash locked away in your shares, the best thing you can do is to batten down the hatches and sit tight. Markets and share prices have a nasty habit of turning up or down without warning. One of the few City sayings that is absolutely true is 'No bell rings at the top or the bottom.'

Simply to keep up with the unchanged portfolio, the active investor will need to make a gain of 17.9% in the second year and a slightly lesser gain in the two ensuing years. Beating the market by that amount is hard work and has to involve the acceptance of a higher level of risk.

If all this sounds theoretical or a case of using selected figures to prove a mathematical point, look at the figures for unit trusts

investing solely in the United Kingdom on October 31st, 1986 in
Money Management. Comparing the trusts' performance over
seven years against an FT All Share Index which has been adjusted
for reinvested income shows that less than one in three unit trust
managers beat that index. Among unit trusts aiming for capital
growth in the UK, the figure was less than one in four. Unit trust
managers may rightly argue that the index does not include the cost
of dealing. Depressing the index by the 5% initial charge that fund
managers levy on unit trusts, a sum larger than any sizeable fund
would have to pay for buying and selling major shares – still paints
the fund managers in a bad light. The majority still show results
inferior to the main performance measure.

The ultimate manifestation of random walk is the blind stab with
the pin. Amazingly enough, it works as well if not better than any
method of active management if the above figures are any guide.
Looking through the same money management list, who would
have predicted on November 1st, 1979 that £1,000 invested in the
MLA General Trust would be worth £7,109 seven years later while
the same sum invested on the same date in the Robert Fraser
Growth Trust would be worth just £1,670. The former achieved a
compound growth rate of 32.3% while the latter struggled to 7.6%.

Countless tests both theoretical and practical carried out in the
United States prove that the blind stab method beats the averages of
professional managers. The most celebrated was undertaken by
reporters on *Forbes Magazine*, an American business journal. Back
in 1967, the reporting staff found themselves on a hot summer
afternoon with little to do. To relieve the boredom they decided to
construct a portfolio by pinning up the stock prices page of the *New
York Times* and throwing darts at it. They ended up with 28 stocks.
They invested an imaginary $1,000 into each. By 1984, they had
turned that $28,000 into $132,000 including reinvested income, a
compound annual growth rate of 9.5%. They had beaten the vast
majority of professional fund managers over that period. They did
not beat investors who moved from stock to stock or fund to fund at
good moments. Equally they did not lose all their money which they
could have done by switching funds or stocks at bad moments.

You might fear that your stabs with a pin end up by giving you a
portfolio of absolute losers, all of which end up in liquidation. That
is a justified fear if you select just one or two shares. Random walk
studies show that you need at least ten shares to have a balanced
portfolio and that between 20 and 25 is the optimum number. If you

have more than that, you do not achieve any improvement in spreading your risk. You just end up with a very complicated tax return. The odds against picking twenty shares that go bust is several trillions to one. These are odds that you can live with. You are more likely to win a first dividend on the treble chance. Clearly, someone who has only enough money at the moment to buy one or two shares cannot take the chance of using a pin. If you are unable to afford the protection of a portfolio, then look at the 'Choose 'n' hold' method described later in this chapter.

Some of the shares you choose will do well. Some will do badly but many shares that underperform will be the eventual subject of a takeover bid or the entry of new dynamic management. For proof, look at the share price records of Woolworth, Guinness, Imperial Group and Distillers over the first half of the 1980s. There is no way of knowing whether and when this will happen, but if it does the effect on your portfolio may be great.

Most of the studies on the random walk method assume that you are able to hold on to your shares for a long period. The largest amounts of money under management are in pension funds where the managers have to look anything up to seventy years ahead to cover the case of the twenty-year-old trainee who lives to be ninety. Many small investors do have long term aims. If you are in your mid thirties with a good job, your objective may be to save for your retirement. On this timescale, the *Money Management* figures based on seven years could be considered a short term exercise – yet it proves that expensive professional management underperforms a broad range of shares chosen at random. Research carried out in the United States when periods of twenty years and longer are used shows a stronger bias towards random selection and long term holding.

Many Shares Game players do not have enough money to buy a diversified portfolio. Others, despite the evidence, may not have full confidence in the 'pick with a pin' method. You may feel that the random walk offers little help if you have to sell one or two shares to raise money (as opposed to selling to reinvest in some other share) although logically, you could pick the shares to sell with a pin. Investors in these categories should look at a modified form of the random walk.

This is 'choose 'n' hold'. The proposition here is that you choose investments either all at the same time if you have the money or acquire them gradually when you see an opportunity. It offers a

wider choice of how you choose which shares to buy and which to
sell when you have to. You can, if you wish, carry out some
elementary fundamental or technical analysis but don't expect to
turn up some undiscovered wonder stock. It retains a cardinal factor
of the random walk – the saving on dealing costs, management fees
and possibly capital gains tax that the long term investor can enjoy.
'Choose 'n' hold' means that you ignore the sort of advice that tells
you to sell a share automatically when it falls by a set percentage –
15% or 20% is often suggested – from its all-time high spot or from
its high point for that year. That would protect you in a falling bear
market but would have meant missing out on most of the UK bull
market that started in January 1975. Few shares have survived since
then without greater falls at one time or another.

Your first task, once again, is to know yourself. What degree of
risk are you prepared to take? Over long periods, additional risk is
rewarded by above average gains. The stockmarket is efficient and
the share price of a risky company adjusts itself to a level which
attracts investors. They will only come in on the basis that there is
something more in the offing than they would get by investing in a
safer stock. If there was not, they would naturally stick with safer
stocks. If you want to minimise your risk, confine your choice to the
top 100 shares. If you have bought some or all of the privatisation
stocks, you are half way there already. Sticking to the top half of
that list will cut your risk even further. If you are prepared to take on
a greater risk, stretch your choice to the shares in the FT Actuaries
Index. You can get a copy of the constituents of that index from the
Financial Times, Bracken House, Cannon Street, London EC4P
4BY for 28p including postage.

There is little point in going beyond the shares in this index. The
risk increases but the reward does not grow sufficiently to compensate for the higher costs of dealing.

Confining your choice to the major shares gives you easier
marketability, a share price underpinned by a dividend yield and in
many cases solid physical assets such as a well-known brand name,
plant and property. These are all items of value. If the existing
management cannot make good use of assets, then others believe
they can. The company will receive a takeover bid.

Selling a share is always more difficult than buying. Investors grow
attached to their certificates especially if they have given a good
return. Both the random walk and the associated 'choose 'n' hold'

strategies are designed to avoid selling simply for the sake of it. As we have seen, selling and buying another share is guaranteed to enrich the broker but you only have a 50% chance of making the right decision (less once you take costs into consideration).

Selling should be confined to those times when you need cash. You buy shares in the hope that they grow in value, not to swap expensively for others. When you need money, look at your portfolio and check on the total value. If you follow the chance theory of the random walk, you can select your sale with a pin. Otherwise, start with low yielding shares that are expensive in price earnings ratio terms in relation to the market and to your portfolio. You might also consider weeding out shares that no longer conform to your acceptable risk/reward parameters. You might have a policy of sticking with market leaders and one or more of your shares might have slipped well out of that group.

If your need for cash is such that you have to sell off a large part of your portfolio which you will not be able to replace – you might wish to buy a holiday home on retirement for example – then you should consider selling all your portfolio as you will no longer be able to enjoy the essential spread of investments. Selling 80 or 90% of each holding will leave you with an expensive to sell rump. Put what cash you have over into a good general investment trust with low management charges. This will restore the spread of investments and allow you time to enjoy your retirement or whatever else you choose to spend your money on. And that is the target of all investment.

Top companies are well researched and covered on a detailed basis by newspapers. If there are problems about, someone will have published those facts. The existence of problems is not necessarily a deterrent. It just means that you will have to accept greater risk.

Fundamental analysis works from the premise that the stockmarket is not efficient. It claims that many shares are either overvalued or undervalued. You sell the first category and buy the second. That holds true not just for the shares in some tiny company that no one has heard about but also for leading shares such as British Telecom, BP, ICI and Glaxo. It relies on the fact that stockmarkets discount the future. The past and the present are of no interest.

Take two companies, International Metals and Metals Worldwide, that are identical in every way. They both announce profits of

£10m after tax for the year. The share price of both stands at 100p. They each have 100 million shares in issue. After tax earnings per share works out at 10p. It then becomes known, either by an announcement or information leak, that International Metals is going to diversify into gold while its rival intends to move into the silver market. Suppose the price of gold is rising and that of silver is falling. The metals analysts at various stockbrokers now have two jobs. The first is to make an instant judgement of what this means for the two companies. How will the market react to the news? They then follow this up with a more detailed study of how the announcements will affect the two companies.

On an instant basis, the market will most probably prefer the company that is moving into gold. The instant stockmarket reaction will be to mark up the price of International Metals. It goes up to 120p. It may also mark Metals International down. Its new share price is 90p. Not only is it taking on a metal that is falling in price, it appears that its management has been too stupid to see the advantages of gold. But is that right? Has the market misjudged in its haste? If both companies turn their metals into jewellery, International Metals might find that fewer people can now afford their products. It may also have failed to find a good jewellery designer because the best person for the job has been signed up by Metals Worldwide who can sell more silver jewellery and for a higher profit on each item because the metal itself is cheaper. The best analyst estimates that International Metals will make £3m additional profit while Metals International will make £2.5m.

Both companies have had to borrow money to finance their diversification moves. Analysts have to work out the effect on each company's balance sheet – the once a year snapshot of a company's financial structure. Neither has borrowed so much that the expansion risks bringing down the rest of their business. That is good news. They then try to forecast how the profits from the new business will relate to the extra interest each company will have to pay to its bankers.

Moving into gold will cost International Metals £20m. Its annual interest bill at 10% is £2m. Acquiring the silver factory costs £12m. Metals Worldwide has to find interest of £1.2m.

The analysts forecast that profits of the original business of both concerns will improve by 15% to £11.5m in the year. They then forecast the profits of both concerns.

International Metals

Original business	£11.5m	
Gold	£3.0m	less
Interest	£2.0m=	
Profit Forecast	£12.5m	

Earnings per share (100m shares in issue)   12.5p

Metals Worldwide

Original Business	£11.5m	
Silver	£2.5m	less
Interest	£1.2m=	
Profit Forecast	£12.8m	

Earnings per share (100m shares in issue)   12.8p

Dividing the earnings by the number of shares in issue to calculate the earnings per share (eps) is important. A company could have paid for expansion by issuing more shares. The shares would normally be given to the seller (vendor) of the new business who could either keep them or sell them in the stockmarket. This would save having to raise a loan and the resulting bank interest charges. Profits would go up but the existing shareholders would have a smaller slice of the bigger cake. Their earnings would be diluted. Using the eps figure puts all calculations on a standard basis. If International Metals had issued 70m shares to pay for the gold facility and not raised a loan, its profits would be £14.5m but eps would be 8.53p.

Analysts then divide the share price by the eps to get the cornerstone of fundamental analysis – the price earnings ratio, abbreviated to p/e or per. The p/e of both companies on the year just past when the shares of both stood at 100p is 10. This is known as the historic p/e and is the figure given in newspaper share listings. But the stockmarket is only interested in the future. It needs to know the prospective p/e which it calculates by dividing the present share price by the estimated eps for the forthcoming year.

With International Metals at 120p, the prospective eps is 9.6. The prospective figure for Metals Worldwide whose shares are now standing at 90p is 7.0. The fundamental analyst now compares those figures with prospective p/es for both the metals sector and the market as a whole. If the prospective p/e of the metals sector is 8.8, the market now finds International Metals expensive and its rival cheap. Has the market overstressed the importance of gold? If it has, the International Metal shares should be sold before others realise this and the price falls. Investors should then buy Metals International. Or is the stockmarket right? Has the analyst missed a vital clue such as the article on International Metal's chief executive in the trade press which mentioned the company's expectation that profits from the new gold facility would rise to £5m in the year after next as the company has signed a firm contract with a top department store. That would change the picture dramatically. The permutations are infinite. The analyst has to sort out the more likely from the fanciful. *(To simplify the situation, taxation has been ignored. Earnings per share are based on after tax profits.)*

A friendly broker is the best source for prospective p/es. A newspaper such as the *Financial Times* will often refer to this figure. Failing this, the historic p/e is a good second best as the share price will adjust to take in new estimates of prospective earnings. But don't mix up the two. For the choose 'n' hold strategy, compare the p/es of companies in the top 100 (or a wider sample if you wish to take on extra risk) with both the sector (banks, breweries, motors etc) and with the market as a whole. The *Financial Times* gives all these figures. If a sector p/e is below that of the market as a whole, select companies that are near or a little above the sector average. If it is above the market as a whole, select companies that are near or a little below the sector average. This should help you to avoid companies with severe problems and hopelessly overpriced companies. If you have enough money or faith to take the random walk, those companies will not matter as they will balance each other out. The object of using fundamental analysis to choose 'n' hold is to aim at good average shares.

Don't forget the lessons from income stocks. Dividends can be an important part of the total return from a share. They are a safety factor.

You can use your eyes. You can see that wine sales have gone up and that beer sales have fallen. Tobacco sales are down. Some stores do better than others. The importer of one make of car must be doing well. Once you have used your eyes, then use your brain and, if you can, that of a stockbroker. Falling sales may mean rising profits. The hard core of cigarette smokers may be prepared to pay a profitable £3 a packet to sustain their habit. But beer drinkers may prefer wine if beer goes up again. The smart busy store may spend a fortune on its publicity and shopfitting. It may make less money than the dowdy shop which has not spent money for twenty years. Trade may be exceptional in your town but awful elsewhere. What you see is not always what you get in share terms.

Technical analysis suggests that you can make buy and sell decisions by studying a graph of a share price or an index. There is a wide variety of methods but the basic message is that there are certain patterns inherent in the rise and fall of most share prices and by studying the graph, they can be predicted. Technical analysts will typically spend all day long over sheets of graph paper, plotting prices, calculating moving averages – the average of the price of a share each day over a certain number of days recalculated each day – and joining up peaks and troughs. Desk top computers have made their life easier but also more complicated as they give a greater choice of methods in presenting a graph.

They also look at how many shares are traded on a given day, a task made easier by the SEAQ system operating since Big Bang. They may add this to their graphs. In its basic form, technical analysis says that people buy shares, hold them and then sell them. The balance between buyers and sellers changes all the time. When buyers are in the ascendant, the share price goes up. When there are more sellers around, it goes down. But neither of these movements happen instantaneously. They build up. The brightest buy first at the bottom and as the message gets round, more and more people buy. There comes a time when all the buyers have been satisfied. No one else wants the shares at that price. The shares have encountered overhead resistance. The share price then flattens out. The smartest sell. The share price falls causing others to sell until it reaches a level – known as a support zone – when buyers are attracted in again.

Chartists recognise certain patterns – many of which have bodily or sexual connotations. There are heads and shoulders, bottoms, penetrations, necklines, double tops as well as geometric shapes such as boxes and flags. There are trendlines, triangles and three box reversals. Some chartists are willing to read the share comment and company results in newspapers. Purists refuse to do so, claiming that they need nothing other than their charts and anything else is an unhealthy distraction. There is plenty of mystique in technical analysis but does it offer better results than pure chance?

Sadly, there is no evidence that charts provide any safer key to the secrets of the stockmarket than fundamental analysis, which at least has the advantage of being understandable by the majority of

investors. While most fundamental analysts stand on common
ground most of the time when they make their recommendations,
chartists often come up with totally contradictory advice from the
same pattern. The buy signal of one is the sell signal of the other.
One problem is changing the scale of the graph and plotting it over a
different period of time can produce a completely altered pattern.

It is back to the acid test. If a system works on a better than
random basis, the information will be known by all and the share
price will adjust automatically. It is true that on occasions the
market has responded to technical tipping. The share has moved in
the direction predicted. Whether this is the skill of the analyst or
simply a self-fulfilling prophecy – someone says buy, the market
does and the share goes up – is a chicken and egg question. That
there are so many theories in technical analysis and that there are
comparatively so few technical analysts at work either in London or
New York suggests that the market as whole does not view technical
analysis highly. As it has been in operation for many years, that
would appear to be a negative verdict. Technical analysts would
claim that they are misunderstood and that investors fear taking
their advice.

7. Looking at what is going on – Guinness: a share in action

'History is more or less bunk,' said Henry Ford, the founder of the Ford Motor Company in 1916. The same is true of stockmarket history. Hundreds of thousands of words are spoken and written on what has happened in the stockmarket. The hope is that they will provide a clear picture of the future, which is the only concern of Shares Game players. The past is rarely of much help and on the occasions when it is, everyone in the stockmarket knows about it. The share price automatically adjusts.

The past does have lessons to offer, however. These do not lie in how individual companies will fare but in how the game is played in the stockmarket where fear confronts greed minute by minute. Using newspaper reports and other information publicly available to all investors, we examine a year in the life of a Guinness share. Guinness was selected because it is a company which makes a product which is easy to understand. It has a high public profile. It was also involved in a number of corporate situations during 1986, the year in question. It was selected before the events of December 1986 which no outside shareholder could have forecast.

The year opens with Guinness shares standing at around 320p. Five years previously, they had been languishing at 50p. In 1981, the stockmarket perceived Guinness as a sleepy brewery company whose main product appealed to fewer people each year. Then new management in the shape of Ernest Saunders was injected. A large variety of non-drinks interests within the group were sold off or rationalised – the euphemism for closure. Guinness became an aggressive player in the takeover game buying first chains of news-agents and sweetshops and then Bells, the whisky group, in a

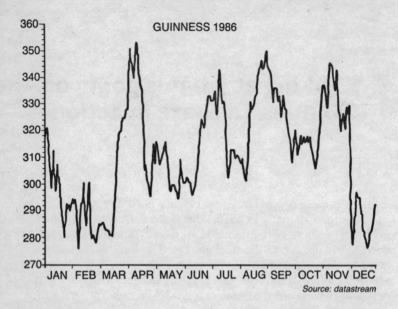

GUINNESS 1986

Source: datastream

particularly hard fought battle. In the eyes of Guinness groupies in the stockmarket and the press, Saunders had become Guinness. Despite a number of clever advertising campaigns, sales of the famous stout failed to show great progress. This did not matter. The perception of the company in the stockmarket had changed. It was no longer the brewer of a famous dark stout popular in Ireland and Nigeria and among older people in Great Britain. It had become a corporate situation, the buzz-word of the period.

January 1986 opens with an explanation of why Guinness shares had moved up during the previous month from 280p. There are rumours that Guinness will be taken over by Beecham, the drugs and soft drinks group. Beecham, it is said, needs to absorb Guinness to make it big enough to ward off the takeover bid that is rumoured to be coming Beecham's way.

January 4th. This story is abandoned to be replaced by rumours that Guinness will make a bid for Distillers, the ailing Scotch whisky group that has already received a hostile bid from Argyll, the Presto supermarket group headed by Jimmy Gulliver, another stockmarket 'hero'.

January 10th. The shares have fallen to 299p. The stockmarket does not like companies which make or are rumoured to be making takeover bids. It is the fear of the unknown. Will the company end up paying too much for its prey? Will it print millions of extra shares to complete the deal? This would flood the market with 'paper' (shares) and disturb the existing balance between supply and demand. News that a rival brewer is edging into the stout market is shrugged off. Stout is not seen as a winner. Some of Guinness's shareholders would like to see the company moving out of stout if it could. (It can't.)

January 13th. The shares move up to 313p ahead of Guinness's profit announcement. The figures are good: better than many expected. But short term speculators taking profits both in the main and in the traded options market push the price down to 300p. (Small investors are often surprised when an item of good news – better than expected profits – forces the shares down and not up. A primary rule of the market is that share prices look forward to the unknown future. Once an announcement is made, it ceases to have any effect on the share price which now looks forward to the next event it can discount. Many of these movements take place before small shareholders even know of the announcement. The figures will be advertised in the newspapers and eventually all shareholders will receive a formal report and accounts for the year.)

January 19th. Leaks to selected Sunday newspapers suggest that Guinness will be a 'White Knight' and ride to rescue Distillers from the clutches of the unwelcome Argyll. Guinness offers 'no comment'. Seasoned Shares Game players can tell from the phrasing of the 'no comment' whether Guinness means yes or no.

January 21st. Guinness bids for Distillers. The shares fall to 293p.

January 23rd. The shares fall to 280p as the market gets wind of a 'dirty' fight. Distillers and Guinness have signed a deal whereby Distillers will have to pay Guinness for its costs if Argyll wins. This is an American tactic known as a 'poison pill'. It makes the target company less palatable to an unwelcome predator.

February 7th. Argyll increases its bid. Guinness shares fall to 285p.

February 15th. The Guinness bid is referred to the Mergers and Monopolies Commission (MMC) because Guinness already has substantial Scotch whisky interests. With Argyll looking 'home and dry', the Guinness price loses 10p.

February 21st. Guinness reveals a deal to avoid the MMC. It will sell parts of Distillers if it wins. It increases its offer and the share price falls 15p to 286p. It then falls to 280p as Guinness becomes embroiled in a row over technicalities of the offer.

March 10th. It is revealed that Distillers' public relations consultants have secretly leaked a letter to selected Sunday newspapers alleging that Jimmy Gulliver had made a mistake in his entry in *Who's Who*. Allegations of other 'dirty tricks' follow including bugging and burglaries. This has little effect on large investors who give little consideration to the rights and wrongs of the conflicting bids but to which bid offers the biggest short term gain.

March 14. Guinness has found a buyer for certain Distillers whisky brands.

March 21st. Argyll counterbids but with Guinness now well ahead – all things being equal, institutions would rather take on extra shares in Guinness than in Argyll as Guinness shares are seen as having more 'quality' than Argyll.

Over the next fortnight, the shares move rapidly upwards to 353p. This helps to convince major shareholders in Distillers that they should opt for the Guinness bid. The rapid rise adding nearly 25% to the value of Guinness has no apparent reason.

April 19th. Guinness wins Distillers. The shares fall 20p to 315p and fall further over the rest of the month as institutions decide they are 'overweight' (have too many shares) in Guinness. By the beginning of May, the shares are just a few pence higher than in mid-March.

June 17th. Half-year profit figures are £4m ahead of forecasts by stockbrokers at £59m before tax. The shares move up 3p to 303p.

July 10th. A stockbroker tells clients in a circular that they should buy Guinness shares. They are 'cheap' at 340p. Other stockbrokers echo this view.

July 13th. A Sunday newspaper, known to support the Guinness board, carries a leaked story which suggests that Guinness will drop its plan to appoint Sir Thomas Risk as chairman. In a circular distributed at the time of the Distillers bid, Guinness said it would appoint Sir Thomas, a director of the Bank of Scotland, to the board. This would help maintain links between Scotland and Guinness, which now owns a large part of the Scotch whisky industry. 'Playing the Tartan card' was an important factor in persuading large Scottish investment trusts and insurance companies to side with Guinness.

July 15th. The 'Risk' story is confirmed. Although it is obvious that Saunders and Sir Thomas have had a disagreement, no one is told why. Wood Mackenzie, Scotland's leading firm of stockbrokers, quit as joint official stockbrokers to Guinness.

July 19th. As the 'Risk' row consumes pages of newsprint, the shares fall from their recent high of 340p to 310p. The amount of beer and whisky sold by Guinness may be up, down or unchanged but fear of what might come out of the dispute gains the upper hand.

August 15th. Guinness sells Distillers' stake in British Petroleum. The shares now stand at 300p. They now start to climb again.

August 23rd. Guinness publishes a circular on why it decided to renege on the promises about Sir Thomas Risk given in the Distillers fight. To minimise impact on the stockmarket itself and to cut down on the expected press criticism, the circular is published at 5 p.m. on the Friday before August Bank Holiday. Guinness will hold an extraordinary meeting so that shareholders can vote on the 'Risk' issue.

August 28th. News that the price of a bottle of Guinness is going up 3p and that the shares will be marketed more aggressively in the United States help the share price on its way upwards.

September 3rd. Guinness rationalises its glass bottle division. It buys out outstanding loan stocks acquired with the Arthur Bell and Distillers takeovers.

September 4th. Unnamed 'major' investing institutions say they will vote against Guinness at the forthcoming meeting, a story that is endlessly repeated in other newspapers over the next days. Many of the institutional shareholders are angry at the way the 'Risk' affair was handled. But their hands are tied as one institutional fund manager admits. Tim Abell, chairman of the Association of Investment Trust Companies told one newspaper: 'Yesterday the AITC said statements must be honoured. But most of my members who are larger shareholders are likely to vote for Mr Saunders and the Guinness board or at worst abstain rather than risk the consequences of a vote of no confidence in the present Guinness board.'

The conventional wisdom that governs these decisions holds that washing dirty linen in public or even worse carrying through a vote of no confidence harms the share price. The duty of these funds is to secure the maximum return for their policyholders and pensioners. Any issues of morality and the future of industry are secondary. Fund managers have to perform well and their ability is measured every three months. If they fail to keep up to standard, their jobs

could be in jeopardy. One conventional excuse for poor performance is to say 'I did what the others did.'

The shares run up to 346p which attracts further 'buy' advice in
circulars from stockbrokers.

September 11th. The Meeting. The morning newspapers report
that a Guinness board victory is a foregone conclusion. Three major
shareholders announce their intention to support the board over the
'Risk' affair just in case there are any other investors still uncertain.
Only one institutional investor makes any serious points against the
board which carries the day by a ratio of 12 to 1.

September 29th. Guinness sells hotels in Scotland.

October 12th. Company announces that sales of bottled Guinness
are rising.

October 15th. Guinness is to get an American Depositary Re-
ceipts (ADR) facility which will make it easier for American
investors to buy the shares. Shares hold steady at around 317p.

October 29th. A broker upgrades its 1987 profits forecast from
£427m to £465m.

November 8th. Restructuring of Distillers and the sale of three
food companies are both announced.

November 12th. More brokers upgrade their profits forecasts. As
the shares move up to 340p, another broker suggests buying on the
grounds that 'the shares should perform well following a dull
period'.

November 20th. A newspaper notes selling of the shares and links
it to 'a bearish circular in preparation at a stockbroker'. The circular
turns out to be bullish.

November 25th. Report of poor Scotch sales in the United States.
The shares are unmoved.

December 2nd. The Department of Trade announces an official
investigation into Guinness following allegations of insider dealing.
The shares fall 35p to 295p and fall a further 9p on the subsequent
day. They now stand at their lowest point so far in the year.

December 3rd. Newspapers suggest that the Department of
Trade will probe a number of dealings in the Distillers bid.

December 10th. Guinness announces its profit figures for the year
to September 30th. It has made £241m before tax with just under
half of that coming from Distillers, whose profits Guinness can
include in its own for the period since the takeover was finalised.
The 'original' Guinness business improved its own profits from
£86m to £132m. Guinness says that there is plenty of growth to come

over the next few years from Distillers. The shares go up 1p to 288p.

In normal circumstances, the full year profit figures would be the most important event in a company calendar. But Guinness is overshadowed by the official probe. This dominates analysis of the results.

December 18th. It is revealed by a leak to a newspaper that Guinness had a secret stake worth $100m in a speculative partnership controlled by Ivan Boesky in the United States. In November, Boesky, a well-known share dealer in New York, had been fined $100m by the Securities and Exchange Commission (SEC) which oversees sharedealing in the United States. Boesky and close business associates had a significant stake in Distillers. They supported Guinness in the bid battle. Guinness shares had recovered to 299p but the latest revelation pushes them down again to 280p.

December 28th. Increasing rumours that large shareholders want Saunders to resign.

Two merchant banks dispute the ownership of 2.15m shares in Guinness purchased for £7.6m at the height of the bid to support the Guinness price. As these shares may be the subject of a DTI probe, no one wants to admit owning them. It is suggested that the purchase may have been in breach of the Companies Act which prevents companies buying their own shares other than in specific circumstances.

December 29th. Guinness shares rise 8p to 289p.

December 31st. Roger Seelig, a director of Morgan Grenfell, a leading City merchant bank and adviser to Guinness throughout the battle for Distillers quits the bank. Morgan Grenfell severs its connections with Guinness. The shares are unchanged. On the first day of trading in the New Year, the shares move up 11p to 300p as bid rumours grow stronger.

Small investors can draw several comforting lessons from this saga.

1. The business of the company – alcoholic drinks – are ignored when the company is involved in a corporate situation such as a takeover bid, a boardroom row or a government inquiry. The day to day affairs of the company including half yearly and annual profit figures are predictable. These results are greeted with little change. If they show an improvement, it will have been reflected in the share price some time previously, especially in a company whose products and sales are as easy to track as those of Guinness. The market only reacts noticeably to surprises.

2. In a corporate situation, the shares move violently but rarely more than a 3% (9p to 10p) movement in one day. None of the moves could have been foreseen by outsiders. But even if you had correctly forecast them, the moves are not big enough to pay for the cost of moving in and out of the shares.

3. Stockbrokers recommend the shares at or near to one of the peaks in the share price graph. There is less enthusiasm for the shares when they sink into troughs.

4. A company that has grown for a number of years is likely to hit a bad patch. This may be from over-confidence which leads to accidents or simply that the idea that powered the company in the first place has run out of steam. Some companies find a new idea. Others decline.

5. In the last days of 1986, Guinness shares were roughly the same price as they had been in the last few weeks of 1985. The market as a whole gained some 20% in the twelve months between those two dates so Guinness would have needed to end the year at around 350p to have kept up. It did not. But it had outpaced the market in previous years.

6. The year started with takeover rumours and ended on the same note. Guinness is rich in assets. It has famous brand names in both the brewing and whisky fields, it has breweries and distilleries and it has chains of newsagents and sweetshops. If, for some reason, the City does not think a board is making a good job of running these assets, it will find another. There may be a takeover – Guinness took over Distillers because the board of the Scotch whisky company had failed to keep the confidence of the City – or as in the case of Ernest Saunders and team's first arrival at Guinness, it may simply be the replacement of one set of directors by another.

7. The market size and assets of Guinness offer shareholders a large measure of protection. Unlike a tiny company quoted on the unlisted securities market, Guinness could not fold up and disappear overnight. Its shares are marketable. A large institutional shareholder can buy or sell hundreds of thousands of shares without unduly ruffling the market. This is especially reassuring if a large shareholder wants to sell. The stockmarket will lower the price but the shares will still find a new home quickly. That would not be true of a small company where the share price could be permanently dented if a large holder decided to sell.

8. Small shareholders can stand aloof from corporate situations. Shareholders in Distillers gained by sitting out the rival bids and waiting until a clear winner emerged. Pledging their shares at an early stage to one or other of the contestants would have been a waste of time. Whatever individual small shareholders might have thought about the Sir Thomas Risk affair, there was little point in their casting a vote. The total of all Guinness shares, its market capitalisation, stands at around £2,500 million. Voting a £1,000 or £5,000 worth of shares will make no difference. The large institutions had a common line. They could not afford to vote Saunders out. If all the small shareholders in the company had voted against the board, it would have made no difference to the final result.

9. The press inflates the importance of corporate rows. They make interesting reading and newspapers have to sell copies. Their effect on the share price over any period longer than a few weeks is minimal.

10. There is always a way out of every situation.

8. Stockbroker Services

Your first share purchase may well have started with an advertisement which said that shares in British Airways, British Gas, British Telecom or the Trustee Savings Bank were on sale. The advert invited you to apply for your share of the shares. You then filled in a very simple form in a newspaper and pinned a cheque to it. The price of the shares was fixed and all you had to do was to multiply the number you wanted by the price. Finally you posted it or if you lived near a receiving bank, you took it in by hand.

Some days later, you received a more complicated document called an allotment letter for a number of shares and perhaps a cheque for a part refund of your money. If you were very unlucky, you would have been sent your original cheque back and no shares. You might also have bought shares in Laura Ashley, Abbey Life or Thames Television in much the same way.

This works well for a new issue – shares which have never previously been traded. Most share dealing, however, concerns second-hand shares which the City prefers to call the secondary or after market. The imaginary story of the merchant ship and its trading trips in an earlier chapter shows that once the initial money is raised, shares go back and forth, up and down, as investors take different views on the chances of the project being successful or failing.

What do you do if you want to buy shares in Tesco? There are no newspaper forms to fill in. And there are strict laws preventing Tesco from selling you shares in the company at the checkout along with your groceries. Equally, Tesco can advertise the quality and the price of its wines or its potato crisps. It cannot advertise the price of its shares and tell you they are worth buying. Once you move on from buying new issues – selling those shares or buying 'second-hand' shares, you need some form of service to handle your purchases and disposals. You cannot just walk onto the floor of the stock exchange and deal.

What service you choose will depend on the amount of money you have to put into shares and what your investment aims are. The amount you have to pay for this service will vary accordingly.

The very idea of paying someone to buy and sell shares makes many potential investors throw up their hands in horror. 'I paid nothing when I applied for my British Gas shares' they say. That is not strictly true. British Gas paid somewhere in the region of £100m for all the various services surrounding its flotation. Publicity alone cost £40m. As an owner of a tiny part of British Gas, each share-holder paid a tiny part of that cost. These costs may be hidden in small print in the full prospectus which you may not have read but they are real and have to be paid. Buying and selling shares in the second-hand market involves you in a retail service. Salaries, rents, telephone charges and other overheads have to be paid in much the same way as any other service.

You also tend to pay for what you get. You expect to pay more in a specialist shop which keeps a wide range of complicated goods and offers free advice than in a supermarket where the workers know nothing about anything. You expect to pay more for a made-to-measure garment than one off the peg. Share dealing services are no different.

In one important respect, you get a fairer deal when you buy or sell shares than when you deposit money in a building society or buy one of many types of insurance policy. When you deal in a share, all the costs involved over and above the amount paid for the shares themselves are shown on the contract note which records your dealings. No building society will break down the cost of each transaction and despite pressure from consumer organisations, it is still impossible to find out the expenses that are built into endowment policy premiums.

Before the City's Big Bang in October 1986, commissions, as dealing costs are known, were fixed. There was a rigid scale which applied whatever level of service you received. It did not matter if you were Joe Public or the Prudential, Britain's biggest investor. Deals in shares worth up to £7,000 attracted commission of 1.65% (plus VAT) and costs of a deal above that was calculated on a sliding

BIGGA & BETTA

Members of the Stock Exchange

1 Bullbear Rd
London

In accordance with your instructions

we have   bought Grand Worldwide Consolidated PLC

by order of   A. Investor

					Bargain date & tax point	Settlement date	Bargain number
					July 1	July 18	123456789
Amount	Price	Consideration	Stamp duty	Commission	VAT		Total
1000	£0.80	£800	£4	£12	£1.80		£817.80

You are advised to retain this Contract Note for Capital Gains and Value Added Tax purposes, indefinitely.

Members of the Stock Exchange

scale which all brokers followed. This was widely perceived as unfair. Clients who demanded complicated services paid the same as those who simply wanted someone to sell their British Telecom shares. Institutional clients such as pension funds felt that the commission they were paying on a £100,000 deal in ICI – a little over £500 – was out of all proportion to the £16.50 paid by a small investor on a £1,000 deal. After all, they reasoned, there was no extra work involved other than putting two more noughts on the paperwork. These big clients were able to vote with their feet – and they did. They dealt in British shares at lower cost in New York. On many days the amount of dealing in ICI, Glaxo or Jaguar was more extensive in New York than in London.

Now it does matter who you are. Big Bang did away with fixed commissions. Now all charges and services are open to negotiation. Although it is too early to forecast how the system will eventually bed down, in the first few months after Big Bang, the Prudentials of the world gained the most. Many stockbrokers halved their commission on big deals to 0.2% or less. Institutional investors can now go direct to market makers and pay no commission at all. They can see all the rival market makers' quotes on their screens.

Small investors did less well. In a few cases, stockbrokers increased their charges on very small deals. In many cases, the old scale was kept and other brokers reduced their charges by a small percentage or introduced a low cost minimal service structure. This was still better than many had predicted. Charges to small investors went up in many cases in the United States where fixed commissions were abolished in 1975 and in Australia which moved over to a negotiated commission arrangement in 1984.

Stockbrokers did not hold or cut their charges out of altruism. They did it because of fierce competition, encouraged by the post Big Bang opening of the Stock Exchange to outsiders such as the high street and foreign banks – and the new technology which is able to cut the cost of the paperwork connected with share dealing. Banks and building societies with branches on every high street are getting in on the act, part of their plans to become financial supermarkets. The personal investor – thought to be following the dodo to extinction just a few years ago – has now become very much worth wooing.

You are faced with a wide choice of services. Before you decide, you need to make two decisions. You must calculate how much you have to invest both now and in the foreseeable future. Most brokers would prefer a client who has £5,000 now but who is able to invest £3,000 a year over the next five years to one who has £10,000 now but no more in the future. The other essential decision is the level of service you require. To an extent this may be decided for you by your answer to the first question. If you have no more than a thousand or two, your choice is narrow. The simplest service is a dealing or 'execution only'. This is not quite as painful as it sounds. It means that a broker or bank will simply carry out your orders to buy or sell a share. You will be given no advice on the suitability or otherwise of your decision and you will be expected not to ask.

The second service is 'discretionary management'. It is 'execution only' stood on its head. If you enter into a discretionary agreement with a stockbroker, you hand over all your existing stocks, shares and unit trusts together with any other money you wish to invest and let the broker buy and sell shares and other securities for your portfolio without any reference to you. You will, of course, be sent a regular update on the progress or otherwise of your portfolio.

The third is an 'advisory management' service. The broker cannot act without your permission – a phone call (tape recorded, so be careful and be clear) is usually enough. Under this arrangement, you should feel free to contact the broker and discuss your own ideas. However, few brokers will take kindly to you spending an hour on the telephone with them if all that results is a £100 purchase of shares. Brokers are human and have to make a living.

Because you pay for what you get, what you pay may be less important than the level of service. If Broker A has a cheap no-frills execution only service with a commission rate of 1% of the value of the shares bought or sold, a £1,000 deal will cost £10. Broker B may offer a full advisory service at 1.65%. Ignoring VAT, the price difference is just £6.50 or 0.65%. Shares very often move more than that percentage in an hour. If you feel happier with help and you have confidence in Broker B's judgement, the extra cost is minimal and may pay for itself several times over if Broker B saves you from making an expensive mistake. It is a question of balancing cost against service. Many brokers will provide clients with services such as newsletters and annual portfolio valuations even if they do not deal for long periods at a time. However, if your playing of the Shares Game is either too infrequent or too small to interest a broker or if you feel confident enough to take your own decisions without reference to a stockmarket professional (and they vary from the very good to the exceptionally mediocre), then price is

important. It may be all that distinguishes one 'execution only'
service from another.

'Execution only' services come from four directions. The fastest
growing, the most accessible but not the cheapest are on the high
street. The major banks have always provided a simple share
dealing service to their customers. Before Big Bang, the bank had to
pass the order on to a stockbroking firm. The customer paid the full
commission – and a fee to the bank as well. It was expensive,
inefficient and slow, but was still the most convenient way for the
small investor to deal.

Big Bang has changed all that. The leading banks have all set up
stockbroking subsidiaries. Lloyds Bank took the do-it-yourself
approach and decided to build up a firm from scratch. Barclays, the
Midland, National Westminster and the Royal Bank of Scotland all
purchased top stockbrokers to give them a ready made capability.
All the banks realised that the growing interest in the Shares Game
could turn their high street branches into a gold mine. The screen-
based share dealing methods that Big Bang brought in its wake were
a catalyst. The banks no longer had to rely on their local clerical
staff. With electronics, every branch could have the same amount of
market information as a stockbroker's office.

In September 1986, NatWest started a pilot scheme to put
screen-based information in a number of branches. This gives a
range of information including a number of share prices and other
stock market information. At around the same time, the Midland
Bank announced it was also providing screen-based information in a
number of branches. At the time of the British Gas share flotation,
NatWest provided touch-sensitive screens in 250 branches at a cost
of £3m to provide instant up-to-the-minute quotations in the share
from its market-making subsidiary County Securities. If you
accepted the quote, you received an immediate contract note
printed by the computer together with instant cheques for those
selling. Very few people bought British Gas through this service.

The NatWest machine or a variant of it will probably form the
basis of a nationwide series of share dealing outlets. It could
certainly cope with offering a similar service on a wider range of
shares although certain technicalities such as the account system
may prevent it issuing immediate cheques. Lloyds has linked its
Sharedeal to a high interest bank account which comes complete
with an overdraft facility. The Midland is offering special share
services to those who hold its gold credit card. Some of these

initiatives will be more successful than others and the final pattern will not be set until there has been much electronic experimentation and market research. The banks will not all offer the same facilities but the mechanics of buying and selling ought soon to be no more difficult than using a hole-in-the-wall cash dispenser.

The Building Societies are getting in on the act as well. Freed from their former legal restraints, some of the bigger societies have formed various link-ups with stockbrokers to provide screen-based services. The Bristol and West has teamed up with Alexanders, Laing and Cruickshank, the Bradford and Bingley has got together with James Capel to sell Personal Equity Plans and other links are in the pipeline.

The second dealing only service is the plastic route. You receive a card similar to a credit card which has a special dealing only phone number and your own personal number. These services can be identified by names incorporating a combination of the following words: broker, card, share, stock, deal, dealer, dealing, call, line and phone. The first stockbroker in the field was Hoare Govett, one of the top ten institutional brokers, with Dealercall. Although others vary in detail, the general theme is similar.

With Dealercall, you agree a credit limit with the broker. When you want to buy a share, you phone the special number which is kept separate from the firm's main switchboard, give the dealer your order, naming the share you wish to buy and how many you want. The order has to be within the pre-arranged credit limit. The dealer will then tell you the best price that can be found in the market. If that price suits you, then you go ahead and deal. A tape recording is made of the call to safeguard the interests of both sides. The system is much the same if you sell although credit limits are obviously of little meaning. Hoare Govett will not give any advice although they do have a pre-recorded and regularly updated telephone information service. Hoare Govett charges 1.25% on both buying and selling with a minimum charge of £12.50. In common with many others, Hoare Govett encourages clients to deposit cash with them in a high interest bank account linked to Dealercall. Some of these accounts can be linked to loan facilities. The Stock Exchange bans member firms giving loans to clients. Since Big Bang, however, many broking firms have become subsidiaries of banks. The parent bank can provide the loan.

The plastic card route is becoming increasingly competitive. Originally conceived as an austere no frills service, it now attracts a few frills. The Hoare Govett recorded phone message is one. Charles Stanley, a medium sized broker with a substantial private client base, offers Gold Dealing Card. Here the brokerage charge is 1% with a minimum of £10. Besides giving quotes to cardholders who phone in, Charles Stanley will send you a research note on up to three shares chosen from the top 500 UK stocks at a time. Most of these services will eventually send clients some form of regular communication on the stockmarket but none will give advice on the telephone. Sending a mailshot is cheap and effective in keeping client loyalty. It can also persuade cardholders to buy shares they might otherwise have overlooked. Telephone conversations are expensive.

The third route is simply to use a conventional stockbroker and pay the normal costs. This has the advantage that at some stage either you or the stockbroker might consider a different form of relationship. Many stockbrokers are now setting up accessible branches in high streets or in department stores. Quilter Goodison, with its move into Debenhams in Oxford Street, London, was the first. Its open plan shop may be hidden behind the bedding department, but it has proved popular and the pattern is being repeated in other stores and in bank and building society branches by Quilter Goodison and other stockbrokers.

The fourth dealing-only route is through a licensed dealer in securities. It is quite different from the first three which are all provided in one way or another by members of the Stock Exchange. Dealing with a member offers the safety net of the Stock Exchange compensation scheme. If the stockbroker runs off with your money or fails to pay debts, the compensation scheme offers a full return of your money up to £250,000. Using a licensed dealer means you forego this safety net.

These dealers often advertise in newspapers, especially in the wake of a major flotation. The attraction is that dealing is free of commission. That sounds very attractive. And it is true. You deal free of commission because the dealer is making a market in the shares. But free of commission does not mean better or even necessarily cheaper. All that happens is that these dealers quote a wider difference between the price they are prepared to buy shares from the public (the bid price) and the price they sell at (the offer price) than a stock exchange market maker.

If the quoted middle price between bid and offer of a share is 100p, it may mean that the best stock exchange market maker is bidding (buying in) at 99p and offering (selling) at 101p. A seller of 1,000 shares would receive £990 less stockbroker's commission and VAT. The most expensive broker would be unlikely to charge more than £18.78 (based on the old fixed scale of 1.65% plus VAT). That would give you £971.22. Other brokers may charge you less.

A licensed dealer, confident that small investors are selling, may quote you 97p bid to 100p offer. Selling your shares would then net you £970 (there is no VAT in dealing directly with a market maker and paying no commission). This dealer can then undercut official market makers and sell the lot to a big institution. You could, of course, buy these shares at a lower cost than from a stockbroker.

Sometimes this route will be marginally cheaper. But it may not be long before one of their salespeople is on the phone to you with a very persuasive line, badgering you to buy high-risk shares of very doubtful quality. You are outside the stock exchange compensation scheme. The disadvantages of this route substantially outweigh the pound or two you might save.

Having your very own personal stockbroker sounds very grand. Many people who have joined in the Shares Game take fright at the thought of approaching a stockbroker for something more than just a plain dealing service. They believe that stockbrokers are only interested in clients with at least £100,000 and preferably £250,000 or more to invest. There are a few stockbrokers like that in just the same way that some car dealers specialise in selling Rolls-Royce or Ferrari. For every stockbroking firm in that league, there are several who are happy with clients whose investment funds are Ford or Fiat shaped.

The easiest way to find a stockbroker is to look in the Yellow Pages where just after 'Steel Tube and Hollow Section Stockists', you will find the heading 'Stockbrokers'. In the London area, over a page is devoted to this category, less elsewhere. There are stockbrokers from Inverness in the north to Truro in the south. There are also stockbrokers in Belfast, Cork and Dublin and in Guernsey, Jersey and the Isle of Man. Be careful with the Yellow Pages listing, however. Besides foreign stockbrokers who may not be at all interested in British clients, the list also contains licensed dealers who are outside the Stock Exchange compensation scheme. Check that anyone you contact from this source is a member of the Stock Exchange. Do not be fooled by vague statements saying 'Yes, we are share dealers' or naming some other trade body no matter how impressive it sounds.

The Stock Exchange in London will send you a list of stock-brokers near to your home who are willing to accept private clients. The Association of Investment Trust Companies (16, Finsbury Circus, London EC2M 7IJ) publishes a free booklet called 'The Private Investor's Stockbroker List'. This is primarily aimed at potential owners of investment trust shares but it does list the minimum amount that each stockbroker will expect you to have available for investment for both their advisory and discretionary services as well as any specialist investment trust services.

Some of the big brokers in this list want you to have at least £50,000 and preferably £75,000 before accepting you as a client. Some of the big brokers not in the list require at least £100,000 and would be happier with £200,000. Others, including most of those outside London, have a much lower minimum or no minimum at all. This does not mean that they will open an account for you with £1 like a building society. It implies a flexibility. They know they would be fools to turn away anyone with a few thousand now but who is moving fast up the earnings scale or who is likely to inherit money in a few years' time. In the meantime, they might suggest unit trusts rather than a portfolio of shares. They may have their own good reasons for this; it may suit many clients. If this is what is on offer, think very carefully and try elsewhere if you want direct entry into the Shares Game rather than sitting on the sidelines.

Whether you eventually opt for a discretionary or an advisory arrangement, your stockbroker will need to build up a picture of your personal financial position and investment aims. You will be asked to supply a list of present investments including gilts, shares (including any in family or private companies), unit trust holdings, building society and bank deposit accounts. A stockbroker will need to know substantial commitments that you have made – a mortgage – or might make in the near future and some idea of your present earnings and tax position including any capital gains tax problem that could be looming such as the sale of a family business. Equally important are your future spending plans – an impending divorce or sending children to fee-paying schools could change everything – and your pension arrangements.

The stockbroker will also need to know your investment aims and objectives. Are you investing for income, speculation or longterm capital growth or a combination? What degree of risk are you willing to take?

After this conversation, a stockbroker might decide that you are either financially or temperamentally unsuited for the Shares Game. Many stockbroking firms have departments which give advice on other forms of investment such as unit trusts, insurance bonds or currency funds.

Assuming that after such a meeting, you and the stockbroker like each other, you will be asked to sign a client agreement. This is part of the new investor protection legislation. Before signing, try and see one or two other stockbrokers and compare the services and the people on offer. It is worse than useless to have a stockbroker that you dislike.

If you opt for an advisory service, the client agreement will be short and probably a version of a document common to most stockbrokers. It will define how you and the stockbroker can end the arrangement and your mutual responsibilities to each other; the broker has to act as your agent in your best interest; send you any monies due from share sales and provide you with agreed services such as statements and valuations of your portfolio at certain intervals. Your main responsibility will be to ensure that all shares and other expenses are paid on time.

Agreements commonly contain a clause which allows the broker to advise you to buy or sell shares in which the broker has a position as marketmaker or units in a trust which the broker manages without making a prior reference to this material interest. If you do not like this or any other clause, discuss it and, if necessary, strike it out or go elsewhere.

A discretionary agreement can be more complicated. You will be asked to list any investment that you do not want to be purchased on your behalf. These may include high risk securities such as traded options, shares traded on the unlisted securities market, the third market, financial and commodity futures and gold bullion dealings. You may also wish to ban the purchase of shares registered in certain countries – South Africa is the most common demand – or in certain industries. There is a growing band of ethical investors that shun shares in companies involved in armaments, alcohol, tobacco, gambling and South Africa. There are a number of ethical unit trusts of which the Friends Provident Stewardship Fund is the best established. You should also tell your broker if your work would make it illegal or embarrassing for you to be a shareholder in certain companies. All of these restrictions go beyond the general guide-lines on risk and reward. Remember that discretionary services are cheaper to administer and a few brokers will only accept discretionary clients. There is no reason why you could not hand over a part of your portfolio to your broker on a discretionary basis and take decisions on the rest yourself. The part you hand over will normally be aimed at lower risk investments.

Once you have found three or four stockbrokers who are happy to have you as a client, you can then start the selection process. Besides dealing on the stockmarket, a stockbroker should provide four other services

1. Research on a wide range of shares and gilts.
2. Communication with clients to inform them of research findings.
3. Dealing with transactions including the paperwork.
4. Providing portfolio valuations and advice on pensions, life assurance and taxation.

All stockbrokers have strengths and weaknesses. Stockbroking is a people business. You have to find one whose temperament and outlook on life fits in with your own. It is your money that is at stake. So how do you judge whether a stockbroker is good, bad or indifferent? The following portrait of a stockbroking firm may help. Greig Middleton is a medium sized stockbroker. Before Big Bang it was a partnership and each partner had unlimited liability if anything went wrong. Now it is a company but is still controlled by its directors. Its outside shareholders include a Scottish bank, a Scottish investment trust, a German bank and a shipping company. It remains a traditional agency broker and has not joined the ranks of the market makers. It claims it is independent of all outside influences. It has offices in London, Glasgow, Bristol and York.

It claims its speciality is finding shares which produce a good return over two to three years. It discourages the sort of client who wants to move in and out of a share within a few days. Unlike brokers specialising in big institutional deals, it does not have a large research staff.

It relies on its own experience to seek out companies which have a good management, strong financial fundamentals and a viable product. It would claim good knowledge of some stocks but by no means all. No broker can hope to adequately cover the thousands of stocks quoted on the London market. Each week it holds an investment committee meeting and decides on the basis of its research which stocks to add to its buy list and which shares it should advise clients to sell. The emphasis is on the gradual accumulation of wealth, not getting rich quickly. Newspaper takeover stories are discussed. Most are dismissed.

Clients receive a newsletter once every four months with views of the market. Greig Middleton has developed its own computer software, Investmaster, which can tell it exactly which clients hold a particular stock and how many they hold. If a particular share suddenly becomes a 'situation' with an involvement in a takeover or a rights issue, they are able to contact all their clients who hold that stock and advise them. This software also speeds up the production of contract notes.

It produces regular portfolio valuations, giving clients details of the level of capital gains and of dividend income. In addition, it can provide deposit schemes for money that is not invested, tax planning, dealing in gold coins, services for expatriates and mortgages.

In common with many other similarly sized stockbrokers, it looks for clients who have around £10,000. At the moment, it does not charge for additional services such as valuations but in common with other brokers, it is constantly reviewing whether it should join the post Big Bang trend to 'unbundling' costs and making a specific charge for each service.

Services offered by the Major high street banks

Barclays Bank

A simplified dealing and share ownership service is scheduled for introduction on a pilot basis in Summer 1987 under the Barclayshare label. Customers will make their own investment decisions based on information and advice provided by the Barclayshare Centre through information screens at selected branches and a regular newsletter service to clients at their home address. Regular clients will be sent valuations and statements of income and capital. Costs have not been finalised but the bank will keep them 'competitive' by the bulk processing of orders through nominee share registration, a method which has the additional benefit of preventing mailing list companies acquiring your name and address. Barclays will charge an annual fee for this service.

Barclays will continue to offer a traditional dealing service with a wide range of stockbrokers. Barclays owns Barclays, de Zoete, Wedd.

Lloyds Bank

The 'Sharedeal' service features a fixed rate of 1.5% of the value of equities bought or sold. The minimum fee will be £10 which is the commission on a deal worth £667. Deals worth £6,666 or more cost the Sharedeal maximum of £100. Dealing in government securities attracts commission of 0.5% with the same minimum and maximum fees. In addition, there will be a 'bank fee' of £1 for deals between £100 and £200 rising on a sliding scale to a maximum £5 on £500 or more. Deals take place through a panel of 24 stockbrokers including Lloyds Merchant Bank, Lloyds' home grown stockbroking arm. Sharedeal can be linked to a high interest cheque account. Account holders can go 'into the red'.

Midland Bank

The Midland is using a simplified sliding scale. It is charging commission of 1.5% on the first £7,000 of any equity deal, 0.55% on the next £8,000 and 0.5% on any balance above £15,000. With gilts, the rates are 1.0% on the first £5,000, 0.25% on the next £8,000 and 0.125% on the balance above £13,000. There is no 'bank fee'. The minimum charge is £15 and there is no maximum. Midland owns two stockbrokers; Greenwell Montagu and the Birmingham firm of Smith Keen Cutler. Most business will be placed through these two firms but Midland will also use a further 21 independent brokers. These services are available in Scotland at Clydesdale Bank and in Ireland at Northern Bank.

National Westminster Bank

NatWest charges 1.5% on the first £5,000 through its Brokerline service. On the next £7,500, it charges 1.0% and between £12,500 and £25,000, the commission rate falls to 0.5%. There is a sliding scale for larger deals falling to 0.2% on any amount above £250,000 although anyone investing this much in a single share would use a more sophisticated service. The first £5,000 of a gilts bargain is charged at 0.75%, while amounts between £5,000 and £20,000 cost 0.25%. Above that, a sliding scale goes up to £2,000,000 where commission falls to 0.08%. There is a minimum commission charge of £15. These charges are under review and are likely to be reduced. Brokerline is a service of NatWest Stockbrokers which operates as the private client arm of County Securities, the bank's main stock-broking subsidiary.

Royal Bank of Scotland

The Royal Bank of Scotland will buy and sell shares on your behalf at no cost other than the commission charged by one of the stockbrokers on its panel. However, the bank charges 1% for the purchase or sale of gilt-edged stock on the National Savings Stock Register and a similar amount for the sale of unit trusts through trust managers. In both cases, there is a minimum of £5 and a maximum of £15. The bank owns the stockbroking firm of Charterhouse Tilney.

VAT and stamp duty has to be added where applicable. VAT is charged on stockbrokers' commissions and on bank fees or charges. Stamp duty is charged at 0.5% on purchases only. The PTM levy is fixed at £0.60 on all deals over £5,000. It helps to finance the Panel on Takeovers and Mergers (the Takeover Panel).

Example 1. Buying £2,000 of ZZZ International Consolidated at Lloyds

Shares –	£2,000
Commission at 1.5%	£30
VAT on commission –	£4.50
Stamp Duty at 0.5%	£10
Bank Fee	£5
VAT on bank fee	£0.75
TOTAL	£2,050.25

Example 2. Selling £20,000 of AAA Worldwide Machines at the NatWest

Cash received for shares	£20,000
LESS –	
1.5% on first £5,000	£75
1.0% on next £7,500	£75
0.5% on next £7,500	£37.50
Total commission payable	£187.50
VAT on commission	£28.12
Panel for Takeovers and Mergers levy	£0.60
TOTAL RECEIVED	£19,783.78

Example 3. Buying £30,000 of Government Stock at Lloyds

Stock	£30,000
Maximum commission	£100
VAT on Commission	£15
Bank Fee	£5
VAT on bank fee	£0.75
PTM levy	£0.60
TOTAL	£30,121.35

Example 4. Selling £10,000 of Government Stock at Midland

Cash received	£10,000
Less –	
0.5% on first £5,000	£25
0.25% on balance	£12.50
Total commission	£37.50
VAT on commission	£5.62
PTM levy	£0.60
TOTAL RECEIVED	£9,956.28

The examples are not intended to present the 'best buy'. Irrespective of cost, you may find it more convenient to deal with your usual bank.

9. The Stock Exchange Automated Quotations System

You have chosen your strategy, selected your shares and contacted a stockbroker. All that remains is to conclude the deal. The electronic wonders of the Big Bang era have made this speedier and more efficient. All the broker now has to do is to press a few buttons. In most cases, you are told the best deal for buying and the best deal available for selling within a fraction of a second. And you will know whether that quote holds good for 1,000 shares or for 1,000,000 shares.

Before Big Bang, the broker had to contact a dealer on the floor of the stock exchange who would go to the pitch where the share was traded and ask the jobbers for quotes before deciding which was best. Then the dealer would report back to the broker who would then contact you to ask if you wished to go ahead. Big Bang abolished the distinction between the broker who acted as your agent in the market and the jobber who was the equivalent of a market stallowner whose stock consisted of shares and gilts and not apples and oranges. Stockbrokers can now act both as your agent and as market maker, the new description for the stallowners.

The floor of the stock exchange is now rarely frequented. That is bad news for the tourists who used to come and stare but good news for investors. Now thanks to SEAQ – the Stock Exchange Automated Quotations System – each broker has constantly updated details of bid and offer prices on a television screen. Even better, SEAQ is available to non-members of the stock exchange. Large investing institutions have SEAQ in their office and often deal directly with the best market maker cutting out commission altogether. Other than cost, there is nothing to stop anyone having

SEAQ in their front room. In one form or another, it will certainly appear in the high street once current plans by banks, building societies and other financial institutions to set up share shops are completed. Big Bang has made the cosy world of the stock exchange public.

This public gaze provides an all important element of investor protection. Under the old system, if you wanted to buy 500 shares of Triple Z Oil and Mineral, the broker would ask the dealer to find out what prices the jobbers were making. The dealer would be careful not to reveal whether the client wanted to buy or sell – advice that remains valid if you deal directly with a market maker whether it is a subsidiary of a high street bank or one of the fringe dealers in the over the counter shares. It would then have been difficult to detect whether the broker came back to you with the best price or not. Now, with SEAQ, all information is in the public domain and all deals are electronically logged. A broker who acts as your agent has a legal obligation under the Financial Services Act to obtain the 'best execution' price for you.

SEAQ splits shares in three categories known by the Greek letters, alpha, beta and gamma. Alpha stocks consist of the eighty or so most traded shares. The next 500 are classed beta. These two groups account for well over 90% of all stockmarket trading. Another 2,000 stocks are in the gamma group. All other shares are in the delta category. Delta shares are traded so rarely that it would be uneconomic to carry details on SEAQ. Shares can be promoted and demoted according to the amount of activity.

The SEAQ screen display for an alpha share is the most informative. The top line gives the time and the SEAQ page number. The second line gives the name of the share and its abbreviated version. The letter 'A' warns brokers that the company has made an announcement today while 'X' informs that the share is ex-dividend, ex-rights or ex-capitalisation. The number at the end of that line is the closing price the night before. The third line carries the volume of shares both bought and sold that day and the prices at which the latest deals were struck. Only the last figure is shown to save space so the display reads, 365½p, 361p, 365p etc. It does not show whether those shares were bought or sold but that is not hard to work out. Shares were bought from investors at 361p and sold at 365p.

The fourth line, which is highlighted, shows the best bid and offer prices known as the 'touch'. The three market makers identified by

SEAQ COMPETING QUOTES   7236 7 10 35

BCHM A

1 2m $365\frac{1}{2}$ 1 5 6 1 6L 5 4   15 23

MGSE SBRO WMAC 361-5 SBRO LANG PBSE

AITC	360-$365\frac{1}{2}$	1×1	JCEA	360-366	1×1
ARPM	$360\frac{1}{2}$-$65\frac{1}{2}$	3×3	LANG	360-365	1×3
			MGSE	361-$365\frac{1}{2}$	2×1
CBIS	360-366	2×3	PBSE	$360\frac{1}{2}$-365	1×1
COML	360-$365\frac{1}{2}$	1×1	PAND	360-366	2×1
CHAS	360-366	1×1	SBRO	361-365	5×5
GWEL	$360\frac{1}{2}$-366	2×1	SCVE	360-366	1×1
HOAR	361-365	1×1	WMAC	361-366	3×3

Southern Bus.Grp. Intm Results.*360#

their abbreviations on the left are the best bid prices for brokers selling their client's shares, in this case 361p. On the right are the three market makers with the best offer prices for clients wanting to buy Beecham. The 'touch' here is 365p. If there are more than three best buys, the three longest standing receive prominence. This prevents less generous market makers following on. The automatic selection of the 'touch' will take on a greater importance when the Stock Exchange's plan to execute small orders automatically with the best market maker is finalised.

Below that are the quotes of all the registered market makers in Beecham. Since Big Bang there are 16 market makers as opposed to three or four jobbers under the old system. Each market maker quotes bid and offer (increasingly known as 'ask' following the American practice) prices. These prices represent a firm commitment to deal and market makers cannot change their mind once interest is shown in a share.

Brokers have to know the 'quote size' – how many shares market makers are prepared to deal in at the quoted price. The bid and offer prices for larger amounts are determined by a fine application of the laws of supply and demand. The 'quote size' is shown by the figures after the prices. Everything is quoted in thousands so that '2 × 3' means that the market maker will bid for 2,000 shares at the quoted price and offer 3,000 shares. In action, a SEAQ screen will often display quote sizes of 100,000 and more.

Beta prices are also firm. There are usually less market makers and the line showing volume and recent trades is omitted. Gamma prices are shown in purple which means they are indicative not firm. Market makers are not obliged to deal at the indicated price. It is there to guide brokers. There is no 'best buy' line so your broker will have to use pre Big Bang skills in dealing with the market maker.

There is a simplified form of SEAQ which shows the best bid and offer prices but does not show which market maker is involved. This SEAQ level 1 service is limited to alpha stocks and will probably form the basis of screen based dealing services that will be on offer in the high street.

Neither Big Bang nor SEAQ has yet changed the stock exchange's unique form of settlement – the polite word for payment. With the exception of unregistered new issues of shares in letter of allotment form and government securities, payment to your broker for shares you have bought and payment from the broker when you sell can be up to three weeks after the deal is completed. This is the account system. In essence, it works in exactly the same way as a monthly account with a credit card company. All the debits and credits on your account are calculated and you receive or write just one cheque. Stock exchange accounts usually last two weeks although they can stretch to three weeks over holiday periods such as Christmas and Easter. Settlement day is usually on the Monday week after the end of the account. If you deal in the last two days of the account, you can opt for 'new time' which puts your deals into the next account. Some stockbrokers have allowed their clients to roll over deals from account to account by a system called 'cash and new', although it is not a service that finds much approval with the stock exchange authorities.

Brokers are entitled to charge for both these extra services in much the same way that Access or Visa charge you for extended credit.

There is an essential difference between the stock exchange account and a credit card. If you buy a hi-fi system on credit and decide to take it back to the store, your debit and your credit are the same. The value of the hi-fi system has not changed. Share values change continually. You could buy Consolidated Factories at 300p and find that later in the account the price has moved to 320p. If you then sold, you would receive 20p per share and save on stamp duty and one commission payment. Speculative account traders often buy shares they cannot afford on the account and sell them at the end. If the price falls, they nurse a loss. They are then referred to as 'stale bulls'. Their presence overhangs the shares with considerable selling pressure as they are obliged to sell at a loss. Prices often rise at the start of the account as speculators chance their luck and fall at the end as the same speculators sell to either take their profits or limit their losses. Stock exchange lore says that the long three week accounts over holiday periods are especially harsh on account traders.

If you sell your shares at the start of the account and the price falls, you could buy them back again and make a profit. The shares will not have left your hands and you receive a cheque on settlement day. A further speculative refinement – and one that the stock exchange has tried to prevent – is 'selling short'. You sell shares that you do not have in the hope that the price will fall during the account. At the end of the account you buy them and simultaneously sell them again – a practice known as 'bear closing'. If the price has fallen sufficiently to cover all your costs, you collect a cheque. If not, you either pay out or attempt to 'cash and new'.

Account trading is dangerous. To make money, you have to not only clear the cost of dealing but also the difference between bid and offer prices known as the 'spread' or the 'turn'. Look at the SEAQ screen for Beecham. There is a 5p spread between the two prices so that the share has to go up 5p just to cover the market maker's turn. In a similarly priced gamma share, the spread could easily be 20p. Add in dealing costs and such a share will have to move nearly 10% before you show a profit. Market makers are usually aware of heavy account trading in gamma stocks which can often occur as a result of a tip sheet recommendation and adjust their prices to 'squeeze' speculators and make greater profits for themselves.

Selling short is even more dangerous. If you buy a share, the worst that can happen is that the price will fall to nothing. There is a defined floor. But suppose you sell a share you do not have and the price soars away. There is no defined ceiling for a share price. You could end up with an enormous bill although in practice you would close your position before matters got out of hand.

Some six weeks after you buy shares, you will receive a certificate. The stock exchange has hopes of abolishing certificates in favour of an electronic transfer system known as Taurus. Small shareholders like certificates and the move will be controversial.

The account system itself may well end – for small investors if not for all. Instant settlement would allow the screen based dealing system set up by National Westminster Bank for dealing in new issues while they are still in unregistered allotment letter form to be extended.

Acknowledgement. The author would like to thank County Securities for their patient help in explaining the finer points of market making on the SEAQ screen.

10. Investment trusts

Leaving it all to a professional to manage a portfolio for you sounds like an easy road to riches. It is not quite as easy as it seems. You still face problems central to any investment decision.

You need to choose how you want your money managed. You must be clear that your investment aims and those of the fund manager are the same. Don't forget your tax position. You may also need to make timing decisions – when to buy and when to sell.

These choices can in some ways be more difficult than selecting individual shares. If you decide to buy or sell shares in Nuts & Bolts PLC, you have a lot of information to help you. You will have some idea of whether sales of nuts and bolts are rising or whether prices have had to be cut to meet competition from other companies offering methods of fixing two pieces of metal together such as Stickiglu PLC or the recent far eastern entrant to the market, Weldalotitsu. You may know that Nuts & Bolts PLC has surplus land to sell in an area of high price housing. None of this will ensure that you make the correct investment decisions but it all helps if you follow the fundamental analysis school of thought.

If you buy a unit or an investment trust, you lose these points of reference. Leaving it all to someone else may mean you have a stake – at one remove – in a hundred or more companies. And these companies may be changing all the time. Shares may be bought or sold, holdings will be increased or decreased – all without your knowledge. Annual and half-yearly reports from unit and investment trusts will give some idea of what is being done with your money. If you are unhappy, your only choice is to move on. Staying needs trust and faith.

On the bright side, short of fraud, you will never lose all your money. Unit and investment trusts go up and down in value. They do not go bust. Money has only been lost in fraudulent enterprises offshore and well out of the mainstream. Remember that playing the Shares Game safely means sticking to shares (including investment trusts) which are quoted on the London stockmarket, dealing through a recognised stockbroker. As far as unit trusts go, invest only in those trusts which are authorised by the Department of Trade. Unless you are going to live outside the United Kingdom, there is little purpose in investing in offshore unit or investment trusts (sometimes respectively called open and closed end funds). But if you do so, make sure it is one connected with a recognised UK fund management group.

Investment trusts, unit trusts and insurance bonds are all ways of investing from a few hundred pounds upwards into a ready made portfolio of shares. But although some investment management companies are involved in all three, there the similarity ends. A century of piecemeal tax, investment and company legislation has created countless artificial differences.

Of these three collective investment methods, investment trusts are the closest to the central theme of the Shares Game. They are shares which are bought and sold on the stockmarket in the same way as any others. An investment trust is simply a company whose business is buying, holding and selling shares. In this way, it is no different from a company like Marks & Spencer whose business is buying, holding and selling textiles and food or Imperial Chemical Industries whose business is buying, holding and selling chemicals and oil. The assets of Marks & Spencer are its stores and warehouses, those of Imperial Chemical Industries are its factories and research laboratories while those of an investment trust are the stocks and shares it owns. The quality of the human assets – directors and employees – is vital.

But the stockmarket does not judge Marks & Spencer or Imperial Chemical Industries solely on the value of the assets. That is part of the equation. How the managers plan to use those assets is more important. The same applies to investment trusts. The value of the assets under the control of the trust's managers is just part of the share price equation. Their skill in using these assets is the other.

Investment trusts are by far the oldest medium of collective investment. The preamble from the prospectus of the oldest surviving investment trust, Foreign and Colonial which was formed in 1868 and is now worth around £800m has been often quoted but remains a key to understanding the original purpose of investment trusts.

The Foreign and Colonial trust was set up to 'give the investor of moderate means the same advantage as the large capitalist in diminishing the risk of investing in Foreign and Colonial Government Stocks, by spreading the investment over a number of different stocks'. The appeal of Foreign and Colonial is no longer mainly to the 'investor of moderate means' and now around three quarters of all the shares are held by investment institutions, a figure in line with the other 150 or so investment trusts.

Colonial governments that issue stocks no longer exist and only a small part of the total portfolio goes into foreign government stocks. The objective now is 'to secure for shareholders long term growth in assets per share and regular increases in dividend which will at least match the rate of inflation'. That is a modest assumption which Foreign and Colonial and many other investment trusts have had no difficulty in achieving in the past. But all these fine words leave out a vital part of the investment trust picture – the price at which investment trust shares can be bought or sold. This is subject to the daily ups and downs of the stockmarket. Unlike a unit trust where the price is subject to a strict formula, investment trust share prices rarely reflect the full value of the share portfolios.

Looking at the American title for an investment trust – closed end fund – helps explain this. Once an investment trust has been set up and its shares sold to the original investors, it is closed to all outside influences. It can pursue its chosen course irrespective of the view that the stockmarket has of its shares in the same way that Marks & Spencer sells its goods each day whether the share price goes up or down. It may choose to take notice of normal shareholder pressure at annual meetings and the more subtle pressure that institutional shareholders can bring to bear informally. Alternatively, it may not, a course that may invite a hostile takeover bid.

The price of investment trust shares is solely determined by the balance between buyers and sellers of the trust's shares. The value of the fund itself is not. This gives rise to two figures for each investment trust share. The first is the stockmarket value which can be checked in a newspaper. The second is the net asset value – known as the nav for short. The nav, which can be expressed as so many pence per share or alternatively as a figure in millions covering the entire trust, represents the value of all the trust's assets less any amount which the trust has borrowed. The difference between the share price and the nav is known as the discount if the share price is lower than the nav or the premium if it is higher. It is rare but not unknown for an investment trust share to be sold at a premium. That usually occurs if there is a takeover bid for the trust or if the trust has a number of holdings which the stockmarket considers undervalued.

To work out the discount, subtract the share price from the nav and then express that difference as a percentage of the nav. So if the nav is 100p and the share price is 75p, the discount is 25%. If the share price stood at 125p, then the premium would be 25%. The exact level of the discount will vary from day to day but has shown a tendency to reduce over the past ten years.

On October 31st, 1976 as the stockmarket was still pulling out of its most serious collapse since 1929, the average discount of all investment trusts stood at 42.1%. Three years later, it was reduced to 30.5%. On the same date in 1983, the discount stood at 25.8% and by October 31st, 1985, the average was cut to 20.9. It has since risen slightly as fears have grown over the future course of world stockmarkets. The average hides a wide range of discounts on individual trusts.

As these figures show, the discount tends to magnify movements in the portfolio of shares within an investment trust. The 1976 figure was calculated less than two years after many commentators had boldly predicted the end of the stockmarket. The 1985 figure reflects a very strong share market. When share prices are rising, it is not only the shares in the investment trust's portfolio that rise. It is the shares of the investment trust itself. This gives the holder a double benefit. If the shares are bought at 80p when the nav stands at 100, the discount is 20%. Suppose that in a strong share market the nav doubles to 200p. This could well be accompanied by a narrowing of the discount to 5%. The shares would then trade at 190p. The underlying portfolio has risen 100% – the value to the shareholder (ignoring dealing charges) has risen by 137.5%. When share values are falling, then investment trusts will tend to magnify the poor performance and drop faster as the discount widens.

Within the average figure, trusts with a portfolio in vogue – Japanese shares during much of 1986, Continental European shares during 1985 and American shares the year before – will tend to sell on a lower discount than trusts investing in unfashionable areas.

Trusts investing in gold, minerals and high technology companies have been out of favour during much of the 1980s.

Swings in the discount give investment trust shares a higher risk and reward ratio than you would experience if you could purchase the underlying portfolio.

The discount is a fact of life. Once it was regarded as a disincentive. Now it is seen as positive. It means you can buy a ready made portfolio at a lower price than would be obtainable if it was built from scratch. This adds to their attractions. Many investment trusts have been on the receiving end of takeover bids – both real and rumoured – over the past few years. When this happens, the discount tends to go down and sometimes disappears or becomes a slight premium. Discounts to net asset values happen elsewhere in the stockmarket, most commonly in property company shares. They arise because it would be impossible to sell the whole portfolio to get cash for the assets without their value collapsing. The discount has advantages to anyone building an income portfolio. Suppose that £10,000 of shares produces £500 of dividend income each year. Buying directly into those shares would produce just £500. Now look at what happens to the same £10,000 used to buy an investment trust with the same shares but standing on a discount to nav of 20%. The £10,000 would buy shares to the value of £12,500 which would produce £625 a year in income. Investment trusts have to distribute at least 85% of their income to shareholders.

Investment trusts can also borrow money – known as gearing in the United Kingdom and leverage in many other countries including the United States – and indulge in all sorts of foreign currency transactions. Gearing is advantageous when a market is rising; a problem when it is falling. In either case the interest on the loan can be offset against any tax that the trust would have to pay.

The ability to involve itself in all sorts of currency dealings can often produce a mismatching of currencies and assets. An investment trust may take the view that shares in French companies offer the best stockmarket rewards but equally take the view that the French franc is not a currency that it trusts. It might prefer the German mark or the Australian dollar. It could then borrow one of the currencies that it likes to buy shares in France. If the chosen currency does well either against sterling or the French franc or both, then the investment trust will have made money for its shareholders irrespective of what happens to the French shares.

The combination of a strong stockmarket and a weak currency is far from unknown. The value of the pound sterling has been falling for many years while its stockmarket has generally been on a firm upward trend. If investment trust managers can get both currencies and shares right, then they win twice on behalf of their shareholders and also on their own behalf. Management fees are expressed in percentages of the fund's value. The better the performance, the more the fund management company earns and in some cases, the more the individual fund manager is paid.

Currencies have been a very important part of investment trust management over recent time with changes in the value of sterling against major foreign currencies such as the dollar, the German mark and the Japanese yen often being greater than changes in a basket of shares in the stockmarkets of those countries. Over the year to October 31st, 1986, a German investor on the Frankfurt market using German marks would have seen a gain of 15.9%. A British investor converting sterling into marks to buy the same shares which make up the German stockmarket index and then converting back would have gained 50.7% in sterling terms – more than three times as much. Over the same period, the sterling investor has more than doubled the gain that the Japanese investor would have made on the Tokyo stockmarket and achieved a return some 50% higher than an Italian investor on the Milan stockmarket. The general trend of sterling has been downwards for the past sixty years. This has enabled investment trusts with their large overseas element to outperform both the UK share index and the Morgan Stanley Capital International index which measures the average level of all the world's stock exchanges.

How do you select an investment trust? In narrowing down the 150 or so trusts to one or two for your own investment purposes, the first task is to decide why you are using an investment trust. Suppose you have £10,000 to invest in the stockmarket. You may wish to devote 20% of this money to following your own or someone else's ideas, perhaps in highly speculative situations. Looking after these shares may absorb all your energies. You could then put the balance of £8,000 into a large general investment trust. This would give you a good spread of professionally managed shares which you would find difficult if not impossible to replicate. Alternatively, you might have invested your first £8,000 according to your own tastes and feel that you need some exposure to one or more overseas markets such as Japan or the United States. Here one of the more specialist investment trusts would be useful to plug the gap in your portfolio.

In selecting a trust, the names are rarely much help. Names such as Triplevest, Jos, Witan, Yeoman and Group Investors tell you nothing. And just what is anyone supposed to make out of the Nineteen Twenty-Eight Investment Trust PLC other than it was set up in 1928. Was it a good thing to set up an investment trust as stock exchanges were boiling in the year before the Wall Street crash? Nearly sixty years later, it probably does not matter. It is an investment trust that invests principally into other investment trusts – a sort of portfolio of portfolios – and has not been one of the better performers over recent years. That does matter.

Some names are downright confusing. British Assets has over half its holdings in North America, Foreign and Colonial has a third of its portfolio in the UK while First Scottish American has little in either Scotland or America. Much of this confusion springs from the distant past when the investments of these trusts did have a close correlation with their title. However, many of the more recent trusts have been set up with specific investment objectives such as Japan, the United States, technology companies or the Far East. These investment trusts usually reflect their purpose in their title.

The Association of Investment Trust Companies – the trade body for investment trusts – classes trusts according to present investment objectives and not to their original purpose. The AITC has no less than thirteen categories but for practical purposes that number can be reduced to five: general trusts, capital growth trusts, income trusts, specialist trusts and split level trusts.

General trusts aim at producing an acceptable mixture of income and capital growth for their shareholders. The official AITC categorisation is 'Capital and Income Growth – General'. This takes in most of the very large trusts such as Globe, Foreign and Colonial, Edinburgh Investment, TR (Touche Remnant) Industrial and General and Scottish Mortgage. These six trusts collectively have assets in excess of £4,000 million. General trusts invest anywhere in the world although a sizeable proportion is invested in the United Kingdom. A few trusts in this category concentrate on the United Kingdom – useful for the investor who has little faith in the ability of fund managers to manage foreign currencies.

The level of income produced by these trusts varies from 2% to over 4.5% compared with the average of all United Kingdom shares of 4%. But as they contain substantial proportions of overseas shares, the risk is greater than a portfolio of UK shares of a similar yield. Investment trust performance is judged by the total return of income and capital growth or loss added together. The income is taxed at the basic rate and reinvested to buy more shares. This irons out the differences between low yielding trusts aimed at a high rate of capital return and trusts with higher yields where capital perfor-mance will not be so marked. You own tax position may be different.

The income category is small. It consists of just 10 trusts whose gross yield is above that of the average of the Financial Times All Share Index – anything from 4.5% upwards. Buttressed by their yield, they tend to be safer and their overall total return perfor-mance including both the income and the capital growth has main-tained itself at around the average of all investment trusts – and sometimes above. Big names in this area include British Assets, Investors Capital, Murray International and Securities Trust of Scotland. Their appeal is to the non-taxpayer and to anyone looking for an investment trust share that can be safely locked away for a long period with good hopes of capital growth. Higher rate tax-payers should avoid them – too much of their total return disappears into the Inland Revenue.

Trusts aimed at capital growth pay out small and sometimes virtually invisible dividends. This is advantageous to higher rate taxpayers. These trusts depend on the growth in the share values of their investments for their own progress rather than any stream of income from those shares. As income shares show, dividend flow tends to be a steadying influence on a share price. Its absence produces a more volatile share price – changes are more frequent and more violent. The ratio between risk and reward is higher.

A few capital growth trusts have portfolios split between the United Kingdom and overseas. Anglo-American Securities and Atlantic Assets are the main trusts to adopt that investment route. Included in this category is the small but deliciously named Updown Investment Trust. The majority invest most of their assets overseas although the UK stockmarket is rarely ruled out. Big trusts with a large overseas exposure include Fleming Overseas, Scottish East-ern, Scottish Investment and United States Debenture.

With their portfolios spread out across the world – or at least that part which is safe for investment, do not expect any of these general growth trusts to appear among the top performers. Equally, there should be no fear of them featuring among the also-rans. They represent a good home for your money if you are unhappy about the course of events in the United Kingdom but do not require any appreciable income from your portfolio. Their performance will be more volatile than income trusts or general trusts but their share price graph will not be nearly as violent as specialist trusts.

Specialist trusts put all their investment eggs into one basket. The basket may be labelled with a geographical tag such as Japan, Europe, the United States, or the Far East. A few baskets will carry names indicating that their contents invest in commodity shares (a term that can include coal, oil and gas) or in technology shares. Others invest in small or recently established companies. These are the investment trusts to choose if you can stand the roller-coaster ride. Virtually all the best and all the worst trusts over periods ranging from one month to three years come from this category. Over longer periods, the random walk effect starts to show through. The ups and downs then start to even themselves out.

Owning one of these trusts means that short term investors will have to monitor their investment more closely than a general income or growth trust. You will need to watch both the currency and the stockmarket of the area where your chosen trust operates. If Japan is in vogue as an investment, then everything should be right for it. Its stockmarket will be rising, its currency may well be attractive and the discounts definitely will narrow. Add all these features up and it is not difficult for the share price of a specialist trust to gain between 50% and 100% in a year. But when the roller-coaster hits the top and charges downward, the virtuous circle turns vicious and yesterday's super performer becomes today's dog. Share prices start to fall, the currency tends to become less attractive and investment trusts show their habit of exaggerating trends with a widening discount to the net asset value.

Anyone investing £100 in the average Japanese trust at the start of 1982 would have well over £400 five years later. Although there were ups and downs, computerised share buying programs in the United States as well as international and Japanese fund managers were pouring money into the Tokyo stockmarket over that period. Had you put the same money into trusts specialising in commodity investments, you would have been lucky to have turned your £100 into £150. Not only have commodity prices been weak, countries such as Australia and South Africa which rely on raw materials to a large extent have also had weak currencies and weak stockmarkets. None of this is a guide to the future. Few predicted this outcome five years ago.

Split level trusts, the final class of investment trust shares started off as a bright invention some twenty years ago. In a moment of sheer genius – the City can be very good at thinking up new ways to invest other people's money – someone realised that investment trusts had one enormous weakness. Every investment trust aimed to reward its shareholders with a mixture of capital and income, although the proportions might vary. Why not devise a method of segregating the capital from the income? Then two classes of shares could be offered – pure capital for those whose tax position and investment strategy demanded it and pure income for non taxpayers and non taxpaying funds such as pensions and charities.

So far, so easy. Then matters became more complicated. The Shares Game players who thought up this idea got out their slide rules – desk top computers had not yet been invented – and added in two new factors. The first was gearing. This gave one class of shareholder not just the fruits of their own investment but that of the other group as well. So if the initial capital raised was £10m for the income shares and £2m for the capital shares, the income shareholders would get the income on £12m and the capital shareholders would get the capital appreciation on £12m. They would also suffer the loss on the whole £12m if the investments fell in value.

The second new factor was to give each trust a limited life. There would be a fixed date when the income shareholders would receive the original par value of their shares (much like a gilt) while the capital shareholders would end up with all the other assets. In theory, these assets are to be paid out in cash. That would force capital shareholders – assuming all went well – into a taxable capital gain. When split level trusts near the end of their life, sensible trust managers arrange either an extension or for the trust to be taken over. In either case, capital investors end up with shares and not cash. They have no immediate capital gains tax problem. They can sell the new shares at their leisure.

The difficulty with split level trusts is that they are difficult. Details vary immensely between trusts – some give income shareholders a small part of the capital gain while one trust has had not just two levels but three. They lend themselves to number crunching on the grand scale. Most Shares Game players have an aversion to number crunching. The result is that investors tend to fight shy of split level trusts and if investors stay away, the share price tends to suffer. The income shares are usually bought by pension funds and held until the final date so there is little marketability. Split level capital shares tend to operate on a far wider discount to net asset value than conventional investment trusts. At the end of October 1986, the average discount of all trusts was 21.6% – that of split level capital shares stood at 28.6%.

If you are willing to hold on to a capital share until the final date of the trust, you should do better than owning a spread of investment trusts – and the more income tax you pay, the greater your advantage. Over virtually all periods since 1976, the average of the split level capital shares has outperformed – sometimes substantially – the average of all investment trusts. This has little to do with the investment skills of the managers and much to do with the mathematics of the concept. For some of the split level trusts put most of their portfolio into other investment trusts.

At the end of the 1970s the split level concept was taken one stage further with the creation of the charity split level trust which enables investors to make a contribution to charity without money actually leaving their pocket. The charity, which pays no tax, buys all the income shares. Other investors buy all the capital shares. In common with other split level trusts, both classes of shares have a limited life with a set date to wind up the trust announced when the trust is launched. Suppose that the charity puts up £1m and other investors £2m. The charity enjoys all the income free of tax from £3m secure in the knowledge that when the trust is wound up, it will receive its original £1m back. The other shareholders receive the capital gains on £3m – not the £2m they contributed so that if the investments have done well, they gain half as much again as they would have done outside a split trust. If the investments do badly, they will of course lose more. If this happens, they at least have the knowledge that they have done it in a charitable cause and that they can offset the loss against capital gains tax.

Investment trusts have one further charm. They are much cheaper to manage than an equivalent unit trust. Many large investment trusts cost no more than one third of one per cent of their assets to run each year. And as you tend to buy those assets at a discount, the real cost is even less. By contrast, unit trusts rarely cost less than three quarters of one per cent and often one per cent and more. In addition, many unit trust groups have recently announced plans to increase their charges. One per cent or less does not sound much but if the asset base is increasing, the difference pays for the costs of buying and selling investment trust shares in around five years and adds up to a considerable margin over ten years.

You can buy investment trust shares in exactly the same way as any other share. You can also buy a limited range direct from the management companies in a variety of schemes including a regular savings plan. The first in this field was Foreign & Colonial in 1984. Several other large groups have followed on. They all offer three principal services. There is a monthly savings plan for sums of £25 upwards, a facility for investing lump sums with a minimum of £250 and a scheme for automatic dividend reinvestment. Some limit dividend reinvestment to the income from the trust itself. Others will take in income from your other shareholdings. The Robert Fleming group will invest dividends into any of their investment trusts.

As with all monthly schemes, you get more shares when the price is low and less when it is high. For no more effort than setting up a standing order from a bank account and filling in a form, it gives small investors the chance of building up a sizeable holding over a period with no worries about when the shares should be bought.

The investment trust takes the money from all these schemes and buys shares on the stockmarket at least once a month. You are not guaranteed to get the cheapest price of that month but by lumping the money together, there is a considerable saving on dealing costs. Investing £25 or £100 or even £250 as an individual transaction would be very costly as few stockbrokers would be prepared to act for much less than £10. These investment trust savings schemes are the most cost effective way into the stockmarket for anyone with less than £1,000.

Investors in these schemes are sent a statement each month showing how many shares they have bought, the price they paid and the costs involved with that purchase. You cannot buy a fraction of a share – unlike units in a unit trust – so that any money which cannot be invested is held over until the following month. With each monthly statement, you receive a share certificate. By the end of one year, you will have a lot of share certificates. There is no difficulty with this other than one of tidiness. You can have your certificates consolidated so that all your holdings appear on one certificate.

These schemes cannot be used to sell the shares. Sales have to be made through a bank or stockbroker. But there are no penalties if you wish to sell some or all, stop the savings scheme or reduce monthly payments to the minimum. Non-taxpayers can reclaim the tax on the dividends. The low cost and the lack of penalties if you wish to stop make these schemes a viable alternative to insurance based savings schemes which are more costly and penalise the non-taxpayer.

Investment trusts and management groups that operate this facility include: Foreign & Colonial, Robert Fleming, Globe, Scottish American, Touche Remnant and United States Debenture Corporation. In some cases, the facility is limited to the larger more general trusts in each group. In addition, the Alliance Trust and the Second Alliance Trust have a scheme for the reinvestment of the dividend from the trusts themselves but no regular savings facility.

addresses . . .

Alliance Trust,
64, Reform Street,
Dundee DD1 1TJ

Robert Fleming Investment Management,
25, Copthall Avenue,
London EC2R 7DR

Foreign & Colonial Management,
1, Laurence Pountney Hill,
London EC4R 0BA

Globe Investment Trust,
Electra House, Temple Place,
Victoria Embankment,
London WC2R 3HP

Scottish American,
45, Charlotte Square,
Edinburgh EH2 4HW

Touche, Remnant & Co,
Mermaid House, 2, Puddle Dock,
London EC4V 3AT

United States Debenture Corporation,
GT Management,
8, Devonshire Square,
London EC2M 4YJ

11. Unit trusts

Unit trusts are like Christmas clubs. You put money in and take it out whenever you want. But the longer you leave it, the better. While your money is in the trust, it is pooled and invested according to the aims of the trust. You have no say in any policy decision. Unit trusts are open ended and the managers of a trust might have £1m to invest one day and £10m the next. Unlike an investment trust it has no fixed capital.

Unit trust sales have never been higher. With each month that passes, new companies move into the unit trust field and established companies set up new trusts. There are now over 1,000 individual trusts. At the beginning of the 1980s, there were less than 500.

The greatest growth has been in trusts investing overseas. The ending of controls on foreign investment by United Kingdom citizens in 1979 combined with the strong performance of stockmarkets in Europe and the Far East has seen to that.

During the same period, the number of investment trusts has fallen. Looking at the fundamental differences between the two forms explains why. Although both forms of trusts are methods of collective investment in shares, unit trusts are not shares. The rules which govern dealing in shares do not apply to unit trusts. They can be marketed and some groups have sold themselves so well that few investors have noticed their rather mediocre performance. They can be sold through newspaper advertisements at any time in their life. There is no need to send anyone a prospectus. There is no need for a stockbroker.

Within certain constraints such as the need to warn investors that units can go down as well as up, and that past performance is no key to the future, unit trust publicity is free to make wide claims about the quality of fund management under offer. Magazines and newspapers are eager to attract this lucrative source of advertising. They offer prizes for large funds, small funds, medium sized funds, new funds and established funds. Every fund management group seems to have won an award. Every trust seems to have a praiseworthy feature even if it is of 'in the top ten over the past three weeks' variety.

Unit trusts can be purchased 'off the page' from advertisements. Other outlets include stockbrokers, banks, insurance brokers, licensed dealers and increasingly building societies. These outlets all receive commission at 3% on sales. This is not shown as an item on the contract note. All the costs are built into the offer price, the higher of the two quoted in newspapers. When you sell, you receive the lower bid price. The difference between the two, known as the spread, is around 6.5%. The cost of buying and selling a unit trust is somewhat greater than an investment trust with the gap increasing the more successful the underlying unit trust management has been. There should be no charge to pay when you sell a unit trust although some banks and brokers will impose an administrative fee. You can always sell by sending the certificate back to the management company. However you sell, you will receive the same price.

The other cost factor is the annual management fee where unit trusts are typically three times as expensive as investment trusts. This is deducted automatically.

Most advertisements now quote past performance on an offer to bid basis. This is a fair method as it shows exactly how much money the investor who bought and sold on specific dates would actually receive after the built-in costs are deducted. Quoting past performance – never a guarantee to the future – on an offer to offer basis is less reliable. It ignores costs which can be sizeable and thereby flatters the fund.

Since unit trusts are not shares, there are no independent market makers. Units are given two prices according to a formula laid down by the Department of Trade and Industry. The lower or bid basis price is calculated as the sum which the managers could raise if they had to sell every share in the portfolio at one time. The offer basis price is how much they would have to pay to buy an exact replica of the portfolio. The gap between these two prices can be as high as 14%. Units are usually priced on an offer basis with the bid price some 6.5% below. But if the market in the units is bad, the fund can be put on a bid basis which automatically wipes some 7% from the value of the units. Funds do not tell their investors when they do this. Market making decisions rest not with the stockmarket but solely with the fund managers who can decide when to create or cancel units. There can be no discount to net asset value in a unit trust. This removes the double benefit that occurs in an investment trust of discounts narrowing as the asset base of the trust improves. It also removes the opposite double disadvantage when asset values are falling. Unit trusts are less volatile than investment trusts.

Unit trusts are very clearly labelled. If the trust invests in Australia, it has to stay invested in Australia no matter how bad investment conditions are. A specialist investment trust would normally have escape clauses written into its trust deed. The freedom of the investment trust is a two-edged sword. In the hands of a good fund manager, it is an advantage. In the hands of a poor manager, it is a positive liability.

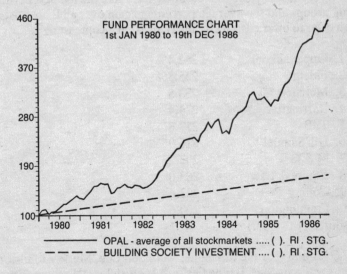

FUND PERFORMANCE CHART
1st JAN 1980 to 19th DEC 1986

———— OPAL - average of all stockmarkets ..... ( ). RI . STG.
– – – – BUILDING SOCIETY INVESTMENT .... ( ). RI . STG.

An investment of £100 in the average unit trust on January 1st, 1980 was worth nearly £460 by the end of 1986. The same money in an ordinary building society account was worth about £160. But although the unit trust price line has moved steeply upwards, there are several occasions when it falls back. The cost of moving out of unit trusts and back again would more than erode any gains you could have made by switching from cash to shares – even if your timing of both your sales and purchases of unit trusts had been perfect. (Source of chart – Opal.)

Selecting a unit trust involves choosing a market and then choosing a fund management group. The Unit Trust Association has no less than 17 categories but for practical purposes many can be ignored. The main choice is whether you wish to invest in the United Kingdom, worldwide, the United States, Japan, the Far East, Europe or into a speciality such as technology or commodity shares. If you choose the United Kingdom or an international fund, you again face deciding between trusts offering low and high dividend yields. The best unit trust statistics are published in the monthly magazine *Money Management* although they are always at least one month out of date. Many brokers subscribe to the Opal or the MicrOpal service which gives instant screen based statistics.

Choosing a fund management company is more problematic. The specialist publication *Fund Management International* publishes monthly statistics showing the overall performance of nearly 100 groups over six months, one year and five years.

Over the five years to December 1st, 1986, the ten best performing groups and the average percentage gain over all their trusts on an offer to offer basis including reinvested income were

1.	Oppenheimer	282.4%
2.	Fidelity	245.5%
3.	Mercury	233.5
4.	Barrington	224.4
5.	TSB	217.8
6.	Hill Samuel	216.9
7.	M & G	203.2
8.	Equity & Law	203.0
9.	County	202.6
10.	Framlington	200.6

(source FMI-Opal)

Over one year the top names were Sun Life, Murray Johnstone, Baring, Eagle Star, Bailile Gifford, Scottish Life, Wardley, Touche Remnant, GT and Life Association of Scotland.

Unit trusts are intended as a medium to long term investment. One factor that does emerge from figures is that choosing the sector is the important factor over periods up to three years. For longer periods, selecting the right fund management group is more vital as the various geographical sectors tend to even out. This is a process that Big Bang and the internationalisation of stockmarkets will hasten as money moves ever faster between countries.

Unit trusts offer the least complicated and the least volatile method of investing in equities. But if you are still confused, several unit trusts portfolio managers will take your money and invest it on your behalf. Some are connected to a unit trust group. They will naturally make their own trusts their first port of call although many will invest up to half your money in trusts managed by rival groups. Most portfolio managers are independent brokers, both within and without the stock exchange, who specialise in unit trusts. But some simply put their own name on recommendations from a unit trust group.

Most unit trust portfolio managers charge an additional annual fee to cover the cost of their work. Their record is far from inspiring according to regular surveys in *Planned Savings* magazine. These show that many failed to match the average of all unit trusts and a number would have fared better had they been left untouched – further proof of the random walk theory. Every switch from one trust to another costs the investor but boosts the earnings of the portfolio manager who picks up a new commission fee although some switches are at discounted rates. The practice of moving money around to collect several fees is known as 'churning', one of the dirtiest words in the Shares Game.

A few unit trust groups offer a special trust which only invests in other trusts in the same group. These are known as managed trusts or more graphically 'funds of funds'. When these were introduced in late 1985, they were roundly attacked by the press although subsequent performance in 1986 suggests that they have performed exactly in line with the average of all unit trusts. The charging basis for these funds is usually higher than an individual trust but lower than a portfolio management service.

12. Overseas

Over 90% of all the world's equities are registered outside the United Kingdom. Nearly 99% of equities are registered outside Australia and even American investors find that 60% of the world's shares are quoted in other countries. Spreading your risk means diversifying outside your home country. Do not be lulled by the long bull market in Britain. It will end some day and for reasons that no one can currently predict. There is some degree of common movement between the various markets of the world but they do not all crash or boom together.

British investors have always known this but were hampered until 1979 by exchange controls. American investors started to get the message in the early 1980s when new pensions legislation imposed penalties on fund managers who performed badly because they ignored non-American stocks and the message has now reached Japan. Big Bang, international equity dealing and the twenty-four hours a day stockmarket all recognise that shares know no frontiers.

Investing overseas is complicated. Risk and reward are both heightened. Wild movements in currencies can often wipe out or double gains or losses on the equities themselves. If sterling falls in value, you do well. This has been the long term trend of the past forty years against virtually all significant currencies but there is no guarantee that it will continue.

Theories of how to invest abroad abound. Some fund managers prefer local expertise to choose stocks while keeping the first stages of the top-down process described in Chapter 15 to themselves. Others believe in the standback concept, doing everything from base. The theory here is that the locals cannot see the wood for the trees.

Risk averse 'choose and hold' investors should have anything between 30 and 40% of their total equity involvement overseas. Pure random walk strategists using a pin ought to include overseas stocks in their selection. There is nothing to stop you buying shares in most overseas companies through a United Kingdom or overseas stockbroker including the many who have set up shop in London. Some overseas stocks are listed on the London stock exchange and prices are quoted in newspapers. In practice, direct investment in shares overseas is impractical. You need at least £100,000 available for equity investment to get sufficient spread. It is often impossible to deal in small amounts on overseas markets. And there is the additional difficulty of settlement, payment of dividends, taxation and the physical delivery of certificates.

More modest investors should opt for investment trusts or for a lower risk but higher costs, there are hundreds of unit trusts investing overseas. Investors with immaculate timing could have

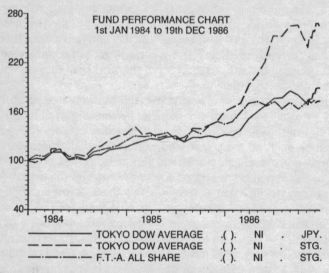

FUND PERFORMANCE CHART
1st JAN 1984 to 19th DEC 1986

————————	TOKYO DOW AVERAGE	.( ).	NI	.	JPY.
– – – – –	TOKYO DOW AVERAGE	.( ).	NI	.	STG.
—·—·—·—	F.T.-A. ALL SHARE	.( ).	NI	.	STG.

Currencies are often more important than stockmarkets. The Tokyo Dow Jones Index (solid line) closely tracked London's FT-Actuaries All Share Index (dash-and-dot line) over the three years to the end of 1986. But adjusting the Tokyo index for the strength of the yen and for the weakness of sterling (dashes line) shows a different picture from autumn 1985 onwards. The currency adjusted line is the test of a UK fund manager's performance. The top down fund manager getting currencies correct will have done well whatever shares were selected. The bottom up fund manager would have to select the very best Japanese shares to do as well. (Source of chart – Opal.)

made a fortune by switching from the United States to Japan in early 1984, then to Europe a year later and back to Japan for most of 1986 before changing to Australia and then back to the United States. Needless to say, no one, least of all professional Shares Game players, was immaculate. With unfettered international money sweeping around the globe at an ever increasing speed, spotting vogue areas at the right time becomes pure chance. And moving in at the top of a market when the unit trust advertising gets frenetic and the panicking out when it falls is a quick route to investment disaster. You should choose four or five investments and stick with them. Over a period, the fast money is incredibly efficient at ironing out differences between markets. Your first investment should be a widely diversified trust which invests anywhere in the world. Follow this with Europe, the Far East and North America. If you still have some money over, try Australia whose natural resources based economy helps its shares to boom while others are flat and Japan which accounts for over 30% of all the world's shares.

Be careful with one country funds in Europe – France, West

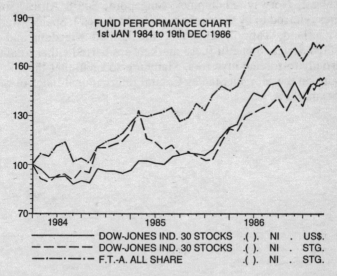

Note the close correlation between the ups and downs of the New York Dow Jones Index expressed in US dollars (solid line) and the FT-Actuaries All Share Index (dash-and-dot line). Currency factors, shown by the sterling adjusted Dow Jones Index (dashes line) provide greater volatility. (Source of chart – Opal.)

Germany, the Netherlands and the Scandinavian countries – and the specialist funds in the Far East covering countries such as Hong Kong, Malaysia, Singapore, Thailand and, on the horizon, South Korea and the Philippines. None of these markets offers sufficient breadth of choice or the depth to withstand a few knocks.

Positively avoid gimmick funds such as 'Portuguese Smaller Companies' or 'Chilean Recovery' – still imaginary at the time of writing but doubtlessly thoughts being nurtured by many a unit trust group marketing department. Markets in smaller countries do boom leading to newspaper headlines proclaiming that Mexico or Austria was the best performing market in the world over the past three months. These booms rarely last and investing in these countries only makes sense if you have enough cash to cover at least ten minor markets.

In all there are 36 countries with stockmarkets active to some degree. They are: Argentina, Australia, Austria, Belgium, Brazil, Canada, Chile, Denmark, Finland, France, West Germany, Greece, Hong Kong, India, Indonesia, Ireland, Israel, Italy, Japan, South Korea, Luxembourg, Malaysia, Mexico, Netherlands, New Zealand, Norway, Philippines, Singapore, South Africa (sometimes referred to by the euphemism 'gold shares'), Spain, Sweden, Switzerland, Taiwan, Thailand, the United Kingdom and the United States. Some of these markets are barred either totally or partially to foreign investors. Many are so small that they do not figure on the Morgan Stanley Capital International Index of world stockmarkets.

13. The Unlisted Securities Market and the Over the Counter Market

The Unlisted Securities Market – the USM – was inaugurated in late 1980 with a motley bunch of companies ranging from speculative oil exploration companies to Fuller, Smith & Turner, a brewery that had been controlled by the same families for over 200 years. It was the Stock Exchange's answer to critics who said it did nothing for small emerging companies.

It allowed companies to obtain a stock market quotation with a shorter track record, less paperwork and at a lower cost than a listing on the main market. Companies can get a USM quote with a three years' record of profit and loss accounts instead of the five demanded on the main market. In certain circumstances, a company with no record whatsoever can gain a quote.

The rules governing what is contained in the prospectus are less demanding. All this makes a USM quote cheaper. But the most important factor is that the directors do not have to sell more than 10% of the company to outside investors. You have to sell at least 25% of the company for a main market quote. This encourages the owners of growing companies to gain a quote without having to sell much of the company that they have built up.

As a method of persuading smaller and younger companies to join the stockmarket, the USM has been a success. There are some 400 companies quoted and a fair number have made the easy step up to the main market. Less than ten have gone bust although a few dozen more are either moribund or have been rescued by other companies for a few pennies a share. Some of these are companies with an apparent bright idea which never quite works out. The shares of Nimslo, a company whose stock in trade is 3D cameras, reached the colossal value of £250m in the early eighties before it had sold one camera. At that time it was worth more than Tesco, which besides selling lots of groceries had many properties in its balance sheet. Sadly, the Nimslo 3D camera failed to sell. Prospective buyers found it expensive and its process unsatisfactory. Since then, the Nimslo share price has been one way – downwards and the company is worth under £10m. Most of the Nimslo investors were the professionals who were eager to buy technological glamour – even if it was untried. Later, they ruefully conceded that they should have known by looking at the name which could stand for Never Invest Money in Such Lousy Offers. Tesco is now worth £1,900m.

The Nimslo story points to one danger of the USM. Shares are volatile. When there was market enthusiasm behind Nimslo, the price moved up very swiftly. Once that evaporated, it moved back even faster. It also shows the danger of the 'vogue concept'. Our chart showing the lack of progress of the Datastream USM index against the FT All Share Index is even more worrying. Whatever might happen to an individual company, the USM as a whole has dragged its feet. The same chart taken back to the start of the USM would show the same trend. The chart contradicts the widely held stockmarket theory that small companies outpace big ones in share price terms in a bull market and do worse in a bear market. The USM has yet to be tested by a bear market.

USM market makers plead that the USM index contains many oil companies and many electronic companies. Both sectors have been poor performers for much of the lifetime of the USM. This illustrates a second danger – that of a market dominated by fashionable concepts which last a short time. The chart cannot show a third danger. Many USM shares are difficult to buy and sometimes even more difficult to sell. The spreads between the market makers' bid and offer (ask) prices are wide. The total percentage cost of buying and selling a USM share is greater than a widely traded alpha stock. A USM share has to move up by 10% or more before you can sell and simply recover your original money, more than twice the gap of alpha shares.

The USM is a volatile market. Shares can and do change their value by 20% and more between the time you open your morning paper and the time you watch the early evening news on television. USM shares are fine if you want to speculate but so far, the rewards have not compensated for the additional risk. They have no place in the portfolios of risk averse investors.

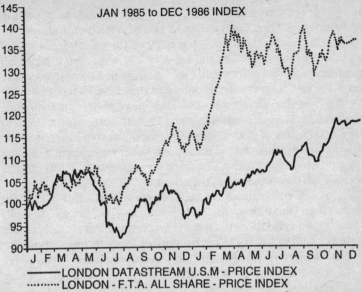

JAN 1985 to DEC 1986 INDEX

———— LONDON DATASTREAM U.S.M - PRICE INDEX
·········· LONDON - F.T.A. ALL SHARE - PRICE INDEX

Source: datastream

USM chart – The main market outpaces the USM

The Over the Counter Market – the OTC – is one of the greatest misnomers in the Shares Game. There is no counter, nor is there any market and as for the 'over', many have suggested that 'under' as in 'under-capitalised', 'under-researched' and 'underhand' might often be more appropriate. The OTC is a loose collection of small marketmakers outside the orbit of the stock exchange and the stock exchange's compensation fund. While most OTC marketmakers trade in mainstream stocks, they make their real money from making a market in the shares of companies too small, too new or too risky to apply for a stock exchange listing.

Most OTC shares are purchased by small investors. Very few professionals are willing to take the risk. They fight shy of stocks where the odds are loaded against the investor and heavily weighted in favour of the marketmaker. They distrust a market where it is far easier to buy than to sell. They dislike a market where there are no requirements governing exactly what goes into a prospectus for a new issue. So should you.

You should remember that an OTC marketmaker is not an independent broker who is acting as your agent and in your best

interest. It is a firm which will may well have a financial interest in
the company it is recommending to you with such enthusiasm. Its
function is to sell you shares – normally on the telephone. Most of
the salespeople employed are paid very low wages but a very high
commission on shares they sell. One favourite line these salespeople
learn is to say, 'Our research shows that these shares should double
in value over the next six months.' This line of patter is meaningless
but the client is impressed. Another is to try to persuade the client to
buy £2,000 worth of shares and then come down step by step to £250
with the line 'If you invest £250, you will either make some money or
you won't lose too much.' The most you can lose is 100% of your
money – whatever the original amount.

Some OTC companies have fined salespeople who buy back stock
from a client who insists on selling. Selling an OTC stock is difficult.
If you do, you should never tell the marketmaker whether you are
buying or selling but try to get firm prices for both transactions for
various amounts of shares before you reveal your hand. If you do try
to sell, you may be given strong arguments to persuade you not only
from refraining but also that you should buy more. The spread
between the bid and the offer prices is often wide – sometimes there
is as much as a 20% gap between the two. However, as you are
dealing directly with a marketmaker, there is no commission and no
VAT.

In some cases, marketmakers admit there is no two-way market
and they will only buy your shares when they can find someone to
sell them to. This is known as a 'matched bargain'. Quoted prices in
newspapers are no more than vague indications of the middle price.
The bid and offer prices will be greatly different. Some prices are
marked 'basis only'. This is an admission that the price is a shot in
the dark and it is up to the shareholder and the marketmaker to get
together and work out a mutually acceptable price.

OTC marketmakers are prohibited under the Financial Services
Act from cold-calling clients. This is the practice of getting a list of
phone numbers and calling up out of the blue with a heavy sales
pitch. There are three ways of getting around this requirement. The
first is to ignore it. If anyone complains, the usual course is for the
OTC marketmaker to say that the cold calling was unauthorised and
the person responsible has been sacked. The second way is to carry
out a transaction in a mainstream stock which legally allows the
OTC company to add the investor's name to its client list. The final
way is to obtain a list of shareholders in a mainstream stock and

offer them a free 'research circular' on that share. The circular may well have some insights although it is more likely to have been put together from newspaper cuttings and old material from stock-brokers. The reply form will include a request for your daytime and evening phone numbers. Once you accept, you will be bombarded with telephone calls selling 'wonder' stocks that are likely to 'double' in a short time. Don't forget that all phone calls are taped.

Many OTC marketmakers have made some efforts to improve their services but a number were either shut down or severely restricted in late 1986 by either the Department of Trade or the Financial Intermediaries, Managers and Brokers Regulatory Association (FIMBRA), the trade body to which most belong.

Everyone involved with the OTC accepts that even under the best conditions, the companies quoted are new, untried and risky. High risk should imply high reward. To make it worth investing in a market where the chances of a company going into receivership is high, investors need to be sure that the average performance of all the shares outpaces that of shares on the main market. Unhappily, for all the talk about the merits of investing in small companies and the isolated examples of OTC shares such as Carborundum which multiplied more than twenty times in value in three years, the overall performance of the OTC has been mediocre.

Each month, the magazine *OTC Investor* plots the progress of new OTC issues over the past three years. With enthusiastic management, a new product and a push from the marketmaker, this should be a period of strong share price growth. Using figures supplied by the marketmakers and ignoring the cost of the bid-offer spread, the *OTC Investor* statistics on October 31st, 1986 show that anyone investing in the top 100 stocks in the main market on any basis would have done better than investing in OTC new issues. There were 42 new issues recorded in 1984. Including Carborundum, four had more than doubled by October 1986. Nine went up but only four by enough to ensure the investor a profit after the cost of the spread and the interest lost by taking the money out of a building society is taken into consideration (OTC shares rarely pay a dividend). Eighteen fell in value including one which dropped by 95% and nine went bust.

Of the 37 new issues in 1985, two gained more than 100%, 13 went up although four failed to clear the spread and the lost interest, 17 fell back and five lost all the money invested in them.

The Stock Exchange has set up a Third Tier market where similar

Don't be afraid of slamming the phone down!

shares would be traded by its own members. It failed to materialise on its planned date in October 1986. It started on a more optimistic footing in January 1987 with a score of companies quoted. The Third Market is partly intended to prevent business leaking away to dealers outside the Stock Exchange. It is also intended as an example of 'forward looking' thinking by the Stock Exchange. The practical effect will be that investors in the Third Market will have greater protection and that the better companies among the candidates for the OTC will gravitate away from the fringe dealers to the Stock Exchange, creating a second layer for the third tier. If the Stock Exchange initiative is successful, it should result in the raising of standards all round. Standards of regulation and disclosure will be less onerous than those on the USM. Companies will be sponsored by stockbrokers who will make a market in the shares of their 'own' companies. Some stockbrokers will also make markets in the shares of other companies.

A word of warning. There are several organisations making a market in obscure shares operating in Amsterdam, Cyprus,

Madrid, Curacao (Netherlands Antilles) and elsewhere who offer 'market letters' and other devices to gain your interest. All are outside the control of the UK authorities. Many of those operating in Amsterdam have been shut down by the Dutch police and most have close links with convicted fraudsters. These so-called 'boiler-room' operations often offer shares in unknown companies which claim to have miracle cures or highly advanced technology. They use highly trained and unscrupulous sales staff who are often flown from Canada (the home of the 'boiler-room') for two month long intensive sales stints. They are paid very well for selling shares. The best way to deal with them is to have nothing to do with them. Put the phone down on them. Make no exception to that rule. Feel no qualms about it. The person at the other end is thick skinned and well used to conversations that end suddenly. Your financial health is at stake. Buying their shares – however enticing they may sound – will almost certainly mean that you lose all your money.

14. Penny stocks

Penny stocks

Penny stocks are the most potent myth peddled at small investors. You may receive a mailshot a week from promoters of one tipsheet or another specialising in low cost shares.

The penny stock legend panders to the British investor's irrational desire to own lots of low priced shares. It has been a long love affair. Promoters of highly speculative rubber, palm oil and tea plantation companies a century ago would price the shares at two shillings instead of the normal one pound. These shares were known as floriners. In the United States, investors happily pay $100 a share (£65), in West Germany, some shares are priced in hundreds of pounds and in Switzerland there are stocks that are so expensive that they have to be subdivided by ten. At £20,000 each, no one can afford them. The British investor would rather have 40,000 shares of 5p each rather than 400 shares at £5.

No one is too sure just what a penny stock is. According to some, it is a share priced at under 10p, to others one that trades under 50p. Whatever, the theory goes that if a share goes up, it will rise by at least one penny. If it is priced at 500p, that is a gain of 0.2%, if it is priced at 5p, the gain is 20%. The mathematics cannot be faulted. Everything else can be.

The share could equally fall by a penny or two. On a 5p share, you have lost a large part of your money. On a 500p share, you would not notice.

The spread on low priced shares is often enormous. If a share's middle price is 5p, the offer price may be 6p. It will have to rise to 7p middle before the bid price rises to the 6p you paid for it. The shares

have had to rise by 40% before you are even back where you started
– and that ignores the broker's commission.

Ask yourself. How would the stockmarket's perception of BP
change if each share costing 700p was divided into 100 new shares of
7p? There is no evidence that penny shares produce any more than
higher priced shares. Selected penny shares perform well as do
selected high price shares. The reverse is equally true.

Much of the recent penny share mythology emanates from Polly
Peck, the overseas trading company with Turkish Cypriot connections. Had you bought the shares at their low of 9p in 1979 and sold
at their high of £33 in 1983, you would have turned £500 into over
£160,000 after dealing costs. But who did? The chances are as
remote as landing three 100–1 winners in a row at a defined race
meeting. But someone may have done it. Polly Peck produced
two 'Turkish' clones. Mellins, a share previously pushed up by
speculators rigging the market in the 1960s, had a run up from 8p to
240p on the grounds of a Turkish managing director. It went bust.
Bellair, a hair lacquer group, went up from a few pennies to £13 in
early 1984 thanks to a Turkish connection and rumours that it was
about to be offered the monopoly for the as yet unannounced
Turkish nuclear power station programme. But the Stock Exchange
froze all further dealings in the shares in early 1984. Its officials
believed that the market in the shares had been rigged – not always
too much of a problem with penny stocks. Bellair shareholders have
been stuck in, unable to sell, ever since. And those who bought
Polly Peck at its peak have since lost half their money. The average
unit trust investing in the United Kingdom doubled over the same
period.

From the top – a look at indexes

Top-down or bottom-up?

Professional fund managers now acknowledge – but only in private – that pursuing the 'right' company to invest in is fruitless. All those hours spent analysing balance sheets and the minutiae of stockbrokers' circulars have been wasted. They now adopt the 'top-down' approach. This method builds a portfolio by starting with the biggest unit in the business world – the economy of an entire continent. 'Top-down' allocates resources to North America, the Far East or to Europe according to a broad brush version of how these respective areas are likely to perform. Fund managers in the United Kingdom include their own domestic stockmarket as a separate category.

Each bloc is then broken down either into individual countries or convenient groupings of inter-dependent economies such as Singapore and Malaysia or West Germany, Switzerland and Holland. The next decision is the currency allocation.

So far, all the decisions have been made on broad economic data. There need not have been any thought given to the stockmarkets of these countries let alone the companies quoted on them. Splitting assets between bonds (government stocks), equities and cash in the respective markets is the next choice to make. Taking the portion assigned to equities, fund managers will then select which sectors are likely to perform well. In Japan, this might start with the choice between companies whose main business is exporting and those who serve the Japanese domestic market. In the United States, fund managers might select between heavy industry such as steel mills,

the so-called 'sunrise' industries such as biotechnology and computer software or service industries including fast food and insurance
broking. Next, they will try to work out how much emphasis should
be given to each sector. What should be the balance between food
retailing and department store shares?

So far, all the decisions can be made against a matrix. The relative
importance or weightings of all the world's stockmarkets are calculated on the Morgan Stanley Capital International Index. The

Country	% of MSCI index
North America	43.5
United States	40.8
Canada	2.6
Mexico	0.1
Europe	23.7
Austria	0.1
Belgium	0.7
Denmark	0.2
France	2.5
Germany (West)	4.7
Italy	2.5
Netherlands	1.6
Norway	0.2
Spain	0.7
Sweden	0.9
Switzerland	2.3
United Kingdom	7.4
Pacific Basin	32.4
Australia	1.3
Hong Kong	0.9
Japan	29.7
Singapore	0.5
Elsewhere	
South Africa	0.32

(source Morgan Stanley Capital International, Geneva./
Wood Mackenzie & Co, Edinburgh)

version on page 132, correct on November 30th, 1986, is based on the average of a basket of world currencies although the index can be recalculated on the basis of the dollar, sterling or any other currency.

Within each country, the relative weightings of each industrial sector are published. The sector analysis of the 732 shares of the Financial Times Actuaries All Share Index in October 1986 was:

Sector	Market Value £m	% of total
Building Materials	7,928	2.96
Contracting, Construction	4,111	1.53
Electricals	1,452	0.54
Electronics	10,313	3.85
Mechanical Engineering	7,545	2.82
Metals & Metals forming	1,314	0.49
Motors	3,598	1.34
Industrial Materials	8,485	3.17
Brewers & Distillers	13,378	4.99
Food Manufacturing	11,916	4.45
Food Retailing	10,110	3.77
Health & Household	15,669	5.85
Leisure	6,500	2.42
Publishing & Printing	4,187	1.56
Packaging & Paper	2,527	0.94
Stores	20,088	7.50
Textiles	3,435	1.28
Tobaccos	6,845	2.55
Chemicals	10,661	3.98
Office Equipment	1,250	0.47
Shipping & Transport	3,575	1.33
Telephone Networks	13,605	5.08
Oil & Gas	25,614	9.56
Miscellaneous	13,875	5.18
Banks	12,779	4.77
Insurance (Life)	6,268	2.34
Insurance (Composite)	7,031	2.62
Insurance (Brokers)	2,721	1.02

Sector	Market Value £m	% of total
Merchant Banks	2,765	1.03
Property	7,303	2.73
Other Financial	3,208	1.20
Investment Trusts	12,558	4.69
Mining Finance	3,185	1.19
Overseas Traders	2,141	0.80

(source: County Securities)

Some professionals have realised that the odds are stacked against them beating the average of the index. So they adopt a technique known as index-tracking – producing a replica of an index and buying and selling according to its twists and turns. This can be computerised resulting in a low cost fund that on past experience should end up in the top half of performance tables. Index-tracking can apply to any index.

The bottom end of the top-down method is the individual stock itself. After the geographical and sector filtering, this now assumes a minor importance.

A few specialist fund managers maintain the older pattern of bottom-up which stresses the individual stock no matter where it is. Their number is dwindling at the moment as more of their colleagues realise the weight in the equation of currencies and national stockmarkets. Bottom-up managers believe that their method will return to fashion one day. It probably will.

Three main indexes track the progress or otherwise of the United Kingdom Stockmarket. All come courtesy of the *Financial Times*. The best known and the most frequently used is the 30 Share index of leading industrial stocks. Assume that this is the index quoted unless you are told otherwise. This is calculated each hour.

The 30 Share index is a good short term indicator but suffers from weaknesses in its statistical construction which can cause inaccuracies over longer periods. If a share in the index went bust, the index itself would go to zero. That does not happen as constituents are changed from time to time. Weak stocks are weeded out and replaced. This index is also incomplete. It ignores investment trusts and property companies and until recently, it also excluded banks and insurance companies.

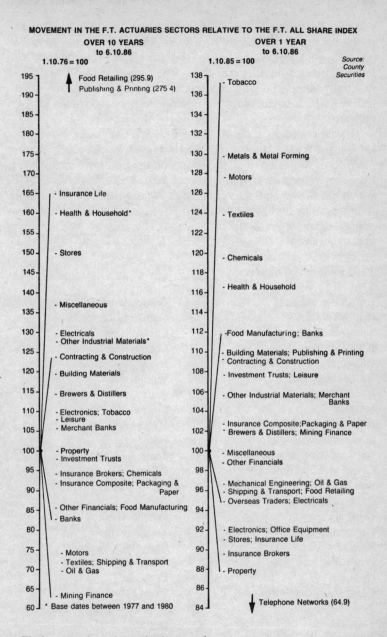

MOVEMENT IN THE F.T. ACTUARIES SECTORS RELATIVE TO THE F.T. ALL SHARE INDEX

OVER 10 YEARS to 6.10.86	OVER 1 YEAR to 6.10.86
1.10.76 = 100	1.10.85 = 100

Source: County Securities

OVER 10 YEARS to 6.10.86 (1.10.76 = 100):

- 195 —
- ↑ Food Retailing (295.9) Publishing & Printing (275 4)
- 190 —
- 185 —
- 180 —
- 175 —
- 170 —
- 165 — Insurance Life
- 160 — Health & Household*
- 155 —
- 150 — Stores
- 145 —
- 140 —
- 135 — Miscellaneous
- 130 — Electricals; Other Industrial Materials*
- 125 — Contracting & Construction
- 120 — Building Materials
- 115 — Brewers & Distillers
- 110 — Electronics; Tobacco; Leisure
- 105 — Merchant Banks
- 100 — Property; Investment Trusts
- 95 — Insurance Brokers; Chemicals
- 90 — Insurance Composite; Packaging & Paper
- 85 — Other Financials; Food Manufacturing
- Banks
- 80 —
- 75 — Motors
- 70 — Textiles; Shipping & Transport; Oil & Gas
- 65 —
- 60 — Mining Finance
- * Base dates between 1977 and 1980

OVER 1 YEAR to 6.10.86 (1.10.85 = 100):

- 138 — Tobacco
- 136 —
- 134 —
- 132 —
- 130 — Metals & Metal Forming
- 128 — Motors
- 126 —
- 124 — Textiles
- 122 —
- 120 — Chemicals
- 118 —
- 116 — Health & Household
- 114 —
- 112 — Food Manufacturing; Banks
- 110 — Building Materials; Publishing & Printing; Contracting & Construction
- 108 — Investment Trusts; Leisure
- 106 — Other Industrial Materials; Merchant Banks
- 104 —
- 102 — Insurance Composite; Packaging & Paper; Brewers & Distillers; Mining Finance
- 100 — Miscellaneous; Other Financials
- 98 —
- 96 — Mechanical Engineering; Oil & Gas; Shipping & Transport; Food Retailing
- 94 — Overseas Traders; Electricals
- 92 — Electronics; Office Equipment; Stores; Insurance Life
- 90 — Insurance Brokers
- 88 — Property
- 86 —
- 84 — ↓ Telephone Networks (64.9)

The long term is no clue to the short term!

The FT-Actuaries All Share Index gets around most of the problems but at the expense of being unwieldy. It has over 730 constituents and is only calculated once each day. It is the favourite index of market number crunchers. The path of an individual share is usually compared with this index or one of its constituent sub-indexes which cover industrial sectors such as electricals or food retailers.

The most recent index is the FT Stock Exchange 100, better known as Footsie. It measures the 100 biggest stocks which account for 70% of the value of all the shares on the London Stockmarket. Like the Acturaries Index, it is weighted. A 5% movement in BP, which has the largest market value in the country, counts for more than a similar 5% movement in one of the smaller Footsie companies such as Royal Bank of Scotland or Jaguar. Footsie is gaining in popularity.

The Leading 100 Shares

British Petroleum	Consolidated Goldfields
British Telecom	Standard Chartered
Shell	Coats Viyella
ICI	Commercial Union
Glaxo	British Aerospace
BAT Industries	Woolworth
Hanson Trust	Associated British Foods
Marks & Spencer	Courtaulds
BTR	Reckitt & Colman
General Electric	Pearson
NatWest Bank	Smith & Nephew
Grand Metropolitan	Pilkington
Barclays Bank	Rank Organisation
Cable & Wireless	Whitbread
Beecham	Legal & General
Unilever	Trafalgar House
Sainsbury	Cadbury-Schweppes
Prudential	Thorn-EMI
Guinness	Ladbroke
Great Universal Stores	Racal Electronics
Bass	British Printing
Lloyds Bank	Jaguar
Allied Lyons	United Biscuits

Rio Tinto Zinc

Boots

Sears

TSB

Royal Insurance

Asda-MFI

Dee Corporation

Tesco

Reuters

Land Securities

P & O

Wellcome

General Accident

Burton

BOC

Fisons

Sun Alliance

Reed

Tarmac

Guardian Royal Exchange

Storehouse

Plessey

Sedgwick Group

Dixons

Trusthouse Forte

Midland Bank

BET

Royal Bank of Scotland

BPB industries

Rowntree Mackintosh

Redland

STC

MEPC

Hawker Siddeley

Bunzl

Willis Faber

Blue Circle

Imperial Continental Gas

Unigate

Rank Hovis

Lonrho

Britoil

Granada

Hammerson

Scottish & Newcastle

Saatchi & Saatchi

British & Commonwealth

Amstrad

English China Clays

Hillsdown

Cookson

Globe Investment Trust

Next

Argyll

(As at October 1986. Source: Wood Mackenzie.)

British Gas would have been placed in seventh position.

16. New issues

Millions have been introduced to the joys of and tears of the stockmarket through the New Issues Game – buying shares when a company makes its first arrival on the shares scene. A company's flotation as a PLC should be the best possible moment to invest. Everything ought to be right. And usually it is. A special breed of city animal, the stag, knows this as well and is rampant when a new issue is around.

You are buying shares in a company which has been expensively groomed by teams of stockbrokers, accountants, lawyers, merchant bankers and public relations people for this moment. The balance sheet will have been spruced up, the products will be shiny, new and in demand and the directors will be overbrimming with optimism and self assurance. They all know that if the first day of trading is a flop, the company may take months to overcome the stigma. Some never recover.

Companies which invite the public to subscribe for new shares have to issue a prospectus. Often consisting of 100 or more pages of small print, they contain information on the company's past trading and financial history, the names and backgrounds of the directors and senior executives, the addresses of directors (increasingly a business address to prevent crime although official returns filed with Companies House show home addresses), their salaries and other financial interests in the company and their own shareholdings. It will contain a balance sheet, possibly a forecast of future profits and dividends and details of the costs of the launch. Most importantly, it will show if the directors and other major shareholders are using the flotation to raise new money or to cash in their own shares by selling them to the public. The latter course suggests that the directors expect you to have more faith in the future of the company than they have. It is reasonable to expect directors to sell some shares but money raised from the public should be used for expanding business – not to provide the managing director with the wherewithal to buy a string of racehorses.

Prospectuses are printed in full in the *Financial Times* and usually at least one other newspaper. They are also available from merchant banks and stockbrokers involved in the flotation. You can request one by post. Many large companies including privatisation companies now issue a 'mini-prospectus' which gives a very abridged version of the full document. A 'mini-prospectus' is short and simple enough to be printed in a tabloid newspaper. Supplies can also be had from banks. You have the legal right to demand a full prospectus if you wish.

Most new issues are launched at a fixed price. The prospectus will state very clearly how much each share costs and whether there will be further instalments. There is no commission to pay but if you submit your application through a broker, the broker may pick up a fee. This will endear you to your broker. Stamp duty is now payable on new issues and it will be built in to the issue price. The application at the back of the prospectus will also state acceptable multiples of shares. There will be a minimum as well. You cannot apply for one share or an odd number such as 1,206 although you would be able to in the secondary market once the share is traded. Unless you apply for a permitted multiple and unless your application form is correct in every other way, it will be rejected. You cannot use photocopied application forms.

Most professionals leave new issue applications to the last moment. Many even go to the extent of getting up early on the final day to hand in their form at the receiving bank before the customary 10.00 a.m. deadline. There is a method in their apparent madness. They want to gauge how well the issue has been received. They listen to City speculation on whether the issue will open above or below the offer price. Newspaper comment and the 'grey market' which allows speculators to deal in shares that have not yet been issued all provide clues. They also look at the general level of the stockmarket. A sudden fall is a danger signal. If they think it is going to flop, they stand clear. Once the form has been received, there is no going back.

If everything looks fine, the stags come out. They are short term investors who apply for many more shares than they can afford in the hope of selling at a profit in the first hours of dealing. Traditionally, stagging involves multiple applications. If the issue is successful, there will be more applications than shares available. It will be oversubscribed. The issuing bank will have to find some way of sharing out the available shares. One method is to scale down applications. The British Gas issue saw big investors scaled down by a greater proportion than their smaller brethren. Another is to hold a ballot which will reject a certain number of applications. Often the two methods are combined. One popular tactic used by the issuing merchant bank is to starve the big institutions of shares. They will all then buy in the aftermarket pushing the shares to a premium. Most merchant banks issuing shares tend to favour the smaller investor. But whatever the basis of allotment, multiple applications give a better chance of success.

Multiple applications are illegal but prosecutions have only arisen in the privatisation issues. It is legal to apply in the names of all the members of your family if they have not already applied. Each individual will have to sign the application form but every cheque could come from your bank account although cheques issued to refund unsuccessful applications will be made out to the applicant and not to you. You can also apply on behalf of your children. The application form will give you details.

Stags take the matter further. They often fill in hundreds of forms using false names and safe addresses, different coloured inks and employing teams of messengers to hand in the forms at the last moment. They have been known to apply for their dogs, cats and goldfish. Some go as far as combing the death notices in newspapers and using the names of the recently deceased. A reliable indicator of a new issue's success is to look through the litter bins in the City. If they are full of prospectuses whose application form has been removed, the issue should go well.

Stags do not read the prospectus. When Stanley Gibbons came to the unlisted securities market in 1984, one newspaper printed an accurate story which accused certain directors of failing to disclose recent company failures with which they were associated. The issue was a success and in the first twenty-one minutes of trading before the stock exchange authority banned further dealings, the shares went to a healthy premium. Whatever the details may bear for the longer term, the stag is only interested in a short term profit. And that will be there as long as there is pent-up demand from other investors.

The first day's premium gives little indication of what happens afterwards. Jaguar opened in 1984 with a 15p premium on the offer price of 165p. Since then the price has more than trebled. In 1985 Abbey Life went to 235p, a 55p premium on the offer price of 180p. A few days later it went up to 250p. Subsequently, despite heavy tipping at the start of 1986, it has traded at far more modest levels. Shares that start at a discount – below their issue price – can eventually recover. It can take a long time.

If you play the new issue game, you must decide whether you intend to stick with the shares or sell out on day one. Stags often have no choice. They apply with money specially borrowed for the purpose or chance their arm by writing out cheques that are backed by nothing in the bank. If you decide to take the quick in and out course, remember that the premiums you have read about in large newspaper headlines may only have held for a few minutes in a hectic market. And don't forget that you will get the bid price, which is lower than the quoted middle price, you will have to pay commission on the sale and that you are losing interest on the money tied up in your application. It can take time to return unsuccessful cheques or part repayments when you have not been allotted as many shares as you wanted.

Add all that together and stagging is not necessarily the free lunch it is purported to be. If you have to borrow money for your application, the arithmetic is further stacked against you. And don't expect the huge premiums in privatisation issues to apply across the board. The government has a political purpose in underpricing these issues.

An offer for sale by tender gets round the problem of underpricing. The mechanism is the same as the sale of a gilt by tender. It leaves little for the stag. You should only apply for these issues if you intend to be a long term holder.

There are other methods of floating a company. Placing shares with selected clients of one or two brokers is a common practice with small companies in the unlisted securities market. Unless you have a connection with the issuing broker, it is best to forget it. Introductions do not involve the issue of new shares. They occur when a company, which is already traded on an overseas market or on the unlisted securities market, seeks a full quotation on the London market.

Successful new issue applicants receive a 'renouncable letter of allotment'. Take great care of this. It is your only proof of share ownership. If it was lost or stolen, the finder or thief might find no difficulty in selling it. You can 'consolidate' several letters together. This is useful if you want to combine family holdings. This saves you from receiving a number of dividend cheques and annual reports. But be careful when there are loyalty bonuses and free gifts such as the British Gas vouchers offered to original shareholders who stay with the stock for a set period. Consolidation counts as a sale – even within a family.

If you hold on to the shares, you will eventually receive a certificate. Your letter of allotment then ceases to have any value.

17. Something extra – rights issues, takeovers and options

Taking the random walk to success in the Shares Game will still involve you in decision making. There will be times when you will be invited to put more money into one of your shares. There will be takeovers – profitable and exciting occasions when you will be invited to sell your shares.

Companies have a choice of ways to raise fresh money. They can go to their bank for a loan. They can join the securitisation craze and raise money by issuing bonds. Or the company can launch a rights issue, printing more shares and selling them at a fixed price, normally at a discount to their market price.

Company law gives existing shareholders pre-emptive 'rights'. They have the first right of refusal if the company is issuing new shares in exchange for cash (although not for property, shares or other assets). If all shareholders take up their rights, all retain exactly the same proportion of the shares. In practice, they do not. Smaller shareholders in particular often ignore rights issues.

The stockmarket will judge a rights issue by its financial terms. This is usually expressed in a formula such as one for three at 100p – shareholders have the right to buy one new share at 100p for each three currently held. The price of the old shares usually falls when a rights issue is announced. A basic calculation is to take the market price of the old shares – say 125p – and work out the value of the rights package. In this case, you would add three old shares at 375p to one new share at 100p and divide the 475p total by four to give 119p. If the price of the old shares settles below that, the rights issue has been badly received. There is a danger that the new shares will end up on the shelf. To avoid that, the bank handling the issue will contact institutional investors in advance to see if they are willing to underwrite the issue in return for a fee. Underwriters guarantee to buy all the shares that are left over in much the same way as they pick up unwanted shares after a flotation. A rights issue is market sensitive information but details often leak out via underwriters and the market adjusts the price before the issue is officially announced.

Reasons for raising the money are often left vague. Phrases like 'for expansion' or 'for future projects' are common. The usual purpose of a rights issue is to improve the company's balance sheet by reducing borrowings. Rights issues are always accompanied by an official circular from the company which will usually contain forecasts of future results. These err on the side of caution. The stockmarket is unforgiving to companies that 'miss' forecasts.

Between the announcement of the issue and the date on which the cash has to be paid, the new shares trade in a 'nil paid' form. You can sell your rights without having to pay for them. In the above example, if the existing shares sell at 119p without the rights issue (known as 'ex-rights'), the new shares should be traded at 19p nil paid (the full price less the cost of a rights issue share). But in practice, they will tend to be a little more expensive. Many share traders like nil paid shares because they can increase their chances of making money by 'gearing up'. You pay a little extra for this.

The arithmetic of 'gearing up' is simple. Put £1,000 into the old shares at 119p and you get 840 shares (ignoring dealing costs). Put the same money into the nil paid and you get 5,263 shares. If the old shares go up 3p, you have made £25.20. If the nil paid go up 3p, you have made £157.90. In the first case, you have not made enough to clear your dealing costs. In the second, you have made a gain after all costs. You also risked losing more if the share price fell. A nil paid rights issue can easily fall to nil pence!

Rights issues are likely to be less common after Big Bang. Many will be replaced by vendor placings or bought deals – two ways of selling huge chunks of shares to institutional shareholders. Companies will have to ask their shareholders for permission to do this as small investors will lose their pre-emptive rights. The advantages of the new methods lie in their low cost and their speed. Rapidity avoids uncertainty. Big brokers argue that most small shareholders are not interested in rights issues. One compromise suggested is to hold back a few shares for interested small investors.

Partly paid shares

Both forms of new issues – flotations and rights – can be sold in a partly paid form. The investor pays one instalment on application and one or more further payments (known as 'calls') on set dates in the future. British Telecom, the TSB and British Gas were all sold in partly paid form. When the second or subsequent instalment is due, investors have either to pay the money or sell the shares. You must do one or the other whatever the price of the shares. Failing to do either means you forfeit your cash and lose the value of the instalment you have already paid. Once the instalment has been paid, the share price will automatically add in the extra. If the partly paid price is 60p and 30p is demanded for the second payment, the price should move to 90p. In practice, it might only move to 88p because many shareholders will sell just before the second call. Some will not have enough money. Others will sell because the call 'gears down' the shares as investors experience the opposite effect to the gearing up seen in nil paid rights. Investors who bought British Telecom at the flotation paid 50p for a partly paid share. The price soon doubled to 100p and trebled to 150p. By late summer 1986, when the two subsequent calls had been made adding up to a grand total of 130p, the shares stood at 180p, a gain of 38.5%. BT shares will have to hit 390p before initial shareholders can again treble their money.

Small companies in high risk areas such as gold mining and exploration often issue partly-paid shares. This gives investors the option of 'pay as you go'. The first payment covers the initial exploration. When the money runs out, the promoters have the choice between abandoning the project or asking shareholders to put up more cash for the next stage. If the company wants more money, shareholders have the option of paying up or giving up their shares.

An alternative and less drastic tactic is to issue warrants along with the original shares which will give holders the opportunity to buy more shares in the future for a fixed sum known as the exercise price. The value of the warrant goes up if the project looks like hitting gold. Warrants, which can come with all sorts of shares but especially investment trusts, offer investors another method of gearing up. The extent of the gearing depends on the exercise price of the warrant and the present value of the share itself. Suppose the share is priced at 100p and the warrant lets you purchase one share at 150p anytime up to 1999. The warrant cannot be exercised (used) as it is cheaper to buy in the market. It is said to be 'out of the money'. But if you bought a warrant at 20p, you have locked to real value once the share price goes over 170p (150p + 20p). You are now 'in the money'. If the shares then move to 250p before expiry in 1999, your warrant is worth at least 100p (250p–150p). You have made an 80p profit and your investment is then worth five times what you paid for it while anyone who bought the shares made a gain of just two and one half times. If there is still some time before expiry, the value of the warrant may be even more if the stockmarket expects the shares to keep going up. Now look at the downside. If the company went bust, the most the warrantholder can lose is 20p. The shareholder loses 100p. The disadvantage of warrants is that they have a limited life. The period to their expiry is an important factor in their value. A warrant near expiry and out of the money is not worth much. Warrants can be complicated. You need a fondness for number crunching.

Takeovers

Takeovers excite shareholders. Unless the news has been leaked or there has been substantial insider trading, they find their shares have shot up in value overnight. But there is nothing magic about a takeover. It simply follows the rule that shares go up if buying pressure is stronger than selling pressure. During the takeover, the bidder wants to buy all the shares. The shareholders know this and hold out for the highest price possible. All the pressure is one way. If a rival takeover or counter-bidder emerges, the upward pressure on the price becomes even more intense. Newspapers like takeovers. They are excited by the clash of personalities if the company under attack fights back. And with many bids now breaching the £1billion mark, they can use the size of headlines to match that sort of money.

Takeovers tend to follow a pattern. Zenith International announces its terms for the acquisition of Nadir Worldwide Consolidated. Zenith can offer cash, its shares or a mixture of the two. It will normally bid for the whole of Nadir although partial bids for an announced percentage of the shares are permitted. Zenith will talk of its bright future and tell Nadir shareholders they will be much better off under the Zenith wing. Nadir slams the terms as unacceptably low and attacks the social consequences of the bid. Counterattacking on the money terms is intended for shareholders whose only concern is whether they are getting a good price. The social effect – employment, inventiveness and the national way of life – is aimed at the media and politicians. In certain cases, a bid can be stopped by the Monopolies and Mergers Commission because it is deemed to be against the public interest.

The offer is roundly condemned by shareholders as mean. In the hope of something better, Nadir shares rise above the offer price. Zenith issues a takeover document which sets out its terms and the first closing date for the offer. When that time arrives, Zenith has only attracted 1% of the shares. No one is surprised. (No one makes up their mind before the final date.) Zenith also has 4.99% built up secretly before the bid (disclosure has to be made if any shareholder has 5% or more) and has bought 3% in the market since the bid was announced. This 3% slice was bought at less than the bid price. Had Zenith paid more, the Takeover Panel which controls bids, would have ordered it to increase its offer to the other shareholders.

Zenith increases its offer. Nadir says that it is not enough – and anyway, the company is not for sale. There are rumours of a second and even higher bid. It arrives in the shape of Acme Investments, a company well disposed to Nadir. Unlike Zenith, which intends to sack the Nadir directors and break the company into small parts and sell them off, Acme intends to leave the Nadir board alone. In takeover jargon, Acme is the 'White Knight' riding to the rescue. Zenith and Acme hold an auction, each threatening to pull out on occasions. Acme offers Nadir the 'poison pill' defence with an option company which can be exercised before the Zenith bid closes. This would take cash out of Nadir and into Acme and leave Nadir a larger and less attractive company than before.

The battle carries on behind the scenes. A director of Acme is friendly with the fund manager of International Insurance which holds 7% of Nadir. They have lunch and International Insurance pledges its holdings to Acme and promises to buy more Nadir shares in the market. This not only gives Acme more shares, it also forces up the price against Zenith.

The Zenith board threatens the directors of the Carey Street Investment Trust with exposure for insider trading during the last Zenith contested takeover unless they back Zenith with their 9% of Nadir. Acme uses its public relations consultants to plant a story in the Sunday Trash which proves that a Zenith director stole a packet of sweets at the age of eleven. Large and small shareholders receive phone calls from the merchant banks acting for Acme and Zenith.

Newspapers are bombarded with views from both sides. Acme and
Zenith both talk of management skills. All the shareholders want to
hear about is the price of their shares. They do not understand
management skills and doubt whether the boards of Acme, Nadir or
Zenith do either.

Eventually Acme wins and Zenith sells its Nadir shares in the
market at a larger profit. The next year, Zenith mounts a bid for
Acme-Nadir. But that is another story.

Not all bids are as eventful. Some are uncontested including
genuine mergers and rescue bids where the shareholders are glad
that anyone wants their stock. Rescue bids often involve reverse
takeovers where a big but badly run company appears to take over a
small dynamic company. The sting is that the directors of the
smaller company take control and pay themselves a generous
amount for their own shares. Shareholders have to watch that their
stock is not being transferred on the cheap. Uncontested and rescue
bids rarely involve cash so you have to be sure that you want the
'paper' of the bidder company and that it is marketable. There is
little that you can do as an individual other than to refuse to sell your
shares, kick up a fuss and hope someone notices. Don't do this
unless you have plenty of spare time and think that it is worth your
while. Shareholder democracy and the fair deal is a fine concept –
but it can consume your time and money. If the company making
the bid gets more than 90% of the outstanding shares, it can move to
acquire your shares compulsorily.

Takeovers tend to come in waves which coincide with strong
stockmarkets as the bidding company will often use its own shares to
buy its target rather than cash. It could not use shares if their value
was low.

Takeover activity exaggerates the upward trend in the market.
But once fund managers start to tire of companies issuing more and
more shares to acquire overvalued companies, takeover activity
declines. The overall level of the stockmarket then weakens. In
1986, the London stockmarket started to fall back once the tide of
'mega-bids' slowed down.

Scrip issues

There is nothing for you to do when a scrip or capitalisation issue is
announced other than wait for a new share certificate to arrive in the
post. A scrip issue, also known as a share split, gives you extra

shares but the value of the shares is diminished. They are normally issued when a share price is getting too 'heavy' – anything over 500p in the UK – although there is no obligation to do so.

An issue will be expressed with a formula such as a '1-for-1 scrip'. For each old share, you get a new share. You now have twice as many shares. It could be '10-for-1' in which case you now have eleven times as many shares. The share price will adjust downwards. In theory, a share priced at 200p will become 100p after a 1-for-1 scrip. In practice, it might go to 105p because scrip issues are usually made when a company is buoyant. The market takes the scrip as a sign of optimism for the future.

Consolidation

Shares can also be consolidated by companies that wish to avoid the penny share image. Four old shares at 20p might be consolidated into one new share. Again, this action is seen as optimistic and the share price might settle down not at the theoretical 80p but a little higher. Consolidation involves often expensive administrative work so it is not undertaken lightly.

Traded options

Traded options are a high risk stockmarket instrument which give you the chance to buy or to sell a share over a set period for a set 'exercise' price in return for a 'premium'. Options are available in many leading shares such as TSB, ICI or British Gas. They operate in much the same way as a warrant except that the period during which an option is valid is no longer than nine months. Options are issued with expiry dates three, six and nine months ahead.

Your investment is geared. If you pay 30p for an option and the underlying share moves 30p in the right direction, you would double your money if you sell your option (less dealing charges and less an element to compensate for the option being nearer to expiry date). If the shares either move the wrong way or never achieve the 30p difference you need, your option is worthless and you have lost all your money.

If you think a share is going to rise, you buy a call option. Otherwise you opt for a put, which allows you to take advantage of a falling share price. The cost of the option is determined by its time value – the number of days before expiry – and the relationship of its exercise price to the actual share price. There are a huge number of technical strategies offered to investors in traded options. There is no evidence that they produce the above average returns that you need to justify a high risk strategy over any period of time. Some are incredibly complicated and demand that you are in touch with the stockmarket on a minute-to-minute basis. There are also tactics on writing options – offering shares you already own at a fixed price for delivery if the option is exercised. If you write options, you end up with the 'premium' cost of the option in your pocket. And if the option is exercised – most are not – you have to dispose of your shares at the agreed price.

Like shares themselves, options offer you unlimited gains but the guarantee that you cannot lose more than your original investment. Your option gives you the right but not the obligation to buy or sell. You can abandon your option as worthless.

In futures trading, you have both the right and the obligation to buy or sell. Futures trading is normally carried out on commodities, currencies and stockmarket indexes such as the FT-SE 100 (Footsie). Your gains and your losses can be limitless. You can limit your losses by the purchase of an option on a future but this is more costly. Futures are traded in New York, Chicago and on the London International Financial Futures Exchange (LIFFE, pronounced life). In the United States, futures trading exceeds share trading in volume. In London, it has remained the province of the professional investor.

Both options and futures can be used to limit rather than to enhance risk. A number of fund managers use them as an insurance policy in case the market moves against them unexpectedly. This is known as hedging.

18. Saving tax – PEPs and the BES

Personal Equity Plans were announced in the 1986 Budget and opened for business in January 1987. Described by the government as a 'radical new scheme', a PEP gives investors the chance to save up to £200 per month or £2,400 each year in a special fund which is entirely free of both income tax and capital gains tax provided the plan is held for a minimum period.

Anyone over the age of 18 can have a PEP. Married couples can have one each. The money has to be invested through a scheme set up by an authorised plan manager who can only accept cash, not existing investments. The cash can only be invested in ordinary shares of companies quoted on the Stock Exchange. This includes companies on the Unlisted Securities Market but excludes gilts, loan stocks, convertibles and warrants. Investment trusts and unit trusts are allowed but only up to the greater of £35 per month (equal to £420 per year) or 25% of the plan's annual value. This gives a maximum of £50 or £600 per year. The investment or unit trust can invest in any stockmarket. Direct investment in shares has to be in United Kingdom companies.

Each plan lasts for one year. During that year, you can keep your investment in cash earning interest which is tax free providing it is reinvested in the plan. After the first year, the plan becomes 'mature' and no more than 10% of the fund can be held in cash. You have the choice each year whether you want to set up a plan or not.

To qualify for tax relief you have to hold the plan for the whole of the following calendar year. Whether you start on January 1st, 1988 or December 31st, 1988, you must hold the plan throughout 1989 and cannot take any cash either from dividends or from the sale of shares until January 1st, 1990 without losing tax relief on the entire plan. Dividends and the procees of share sales have to be reinvested within thirty days.

The PEP scheme is aimed at long term investment with the greatest benefits accruing to investors who aim to hold on to equity investments for a decade or more. It is ideally suited to the two main Shares Game strategies – the 'random walk' and 'choose and hold'. The scheme is not collective investment. Each planholder owns the shares as an individual and can either take the shares out of the plan or take them to another plan manager.

Long term investment and tax relief should add up to a potent attraction. There is another side to PEP, however. And that is the cost structure. Operating a PEP is expensive. Before you take out a plan, you must check to see if the tax relief is worth it or whether having to lock your money away plus the plan charges erode the claimed tax advantages.

For the wealthy investor there is no question. Stockbrokers have written to all their bigger clients suggesting that they either put £2,400 into a plan or sell other investments to raise the cash. If you are rich enough to have a capital gains tax bill each year and pay income tax at the top rate of 60%, PEP is a useful tool. The really wealthy, however, may not notice the savings in the context of their total riches.

For the average person, it is not so clear cut. The first £6,300 plus indexation allowance of any capital gain in any one tax year escapes Capital Gains Tax. You would be very lucky to make enough on your shares to overshoot the free slice and indexation allowance by any substantial amount. Moreover, CGT might either be abolished or radically altered in the future. The income tax relief on dividends is more real. If you are a basic rate taxpayer with the average portfolio yielding 4% gross, you will save £1.16 for each £100 invested in a PEP. Putting your money into a high growth Japanese unit trust would save you around 25p for each £100 – 0.25%.

It would make sense to buy only high yielding investments. In many PEP schemes, that is not possible as investment is either limited to a discretionary service where the plan manager chooses the shares leaving you with no say over the extent of dealing charges or to a limited selection of the most actively traded stocks. Schemes that allow an unfettered choice are either more costly or impose other restrictions.

Charges vary immensely from plan to plan. A number of independent sources produce up to date guides. One of the most Comprehensive is from Chase de Vere Investments (24, Lincoln's Inn Fields, London WC2) whose Pepguide checklist has no less than 25 points for each scheme. The more important are:

* the initial charge to set up the plans
* the annual charge levied on plans in their first and subsequent years
* penalties from withdrawals in either current or mature plans
* the range of investments offered
* the cost of buying and selling shares
* the level of discounts if any on the plan manager's own unit trusts
* charges for attendance at annual meetings and for voting rights

The 'attendance' charge is unique to PEPs. One of the government's aims in setting up PEPs was to encourage active wider share ownership. This included sending investors individual annual reports for all the companies in which they held shares and attendance and voting at annual and other general meetings. Plan managers are obliged to send the reports despite the high cost involved in printing and distributing several thousand extra reports to shareholders who might have no more than £50 in one company. Attendance and voting rights incur even more costs and managers can charge planholders who wish to exercise them. You cannot just go along to a meeting and tell the company you are a shareholder as your name does not appear on the register. There will only be a nominee holding representing all the shares held by the PEP management company on behalf of its clients. Some PEP managers charge up to 10% of the total value of the plan if you wish to attend meetings. At £240, it would be cheaper to buy one share in a company in your own name to ensure your attendance rights. Others make no charge. The very high charges are levied as a deterrent to anyone wishing to claim their rights.

How much will you save with a PEP? With one of the lowest cost plans, the basic rate taxpayer with no capital gains tax problem will save around 1% – and most of that is accounted for by the low cost of dealing in small amounts of shares that some plans provide. Investing £200 in a leading share through a PEP with a major bank will incur brokerage charges of just 0.2% – £0.40 – plus VAT and stamp duty. The commission if the same shares were bought over the bank's counter would be at least £10.

Over the ten years to October 1st, 1986, the average compound annual rate of return on the UK stockmarket including reinvesting income after the deduction of basic rate income tax was 19.7%. One piece of publicity shows that if you had put £2,400 into the stockmarket on that date in 1976 and sold the entire holding ten years later, you would have £14,488. If the entire amount had been in a fund free of all taxes, it would have been worth £22,896 – a gain of £8,408. A top rate taxpayer would have gained even more. But like all statistics, this needs to be treated with a pinch of salt.

These figures ignore charges in the PEP and assume that all the capital gain is subject to Capital Gains Tax. The CGT element accounts for about half the gain. It covers one of the most favourable decades ever in the stockmarket as well as including years in the seventies when the average gross yield on UK shares was around 10%. Basic income tax rates were higher so the savings in a tax free fund were a more significant 3% a year. Compounding the more advantageous conditions for a tax free fund over a long period helps the argument as well.

If the rate of growth had been 12% for a taxed fund and the saving on a PEP plan was 1%, £2,400 becomes worth £7,540 in the taxed fund and £8,147 in a PEP over ten years. At 8% growth in a taxed fund, the sum becomes worth £5,181 and £5,681 in a PEP plan.

The lowest cost PEP plans offer some advantages if you choose a high yielding portfolio of quality shares which you intend to hold for a long period. Other plans can be a positive liability unless you are a higher rate taxpayer faced with a CGT bill.

Whatever you decide, it pays to read the small print carefully.

Investment trust regular savings plans are an alternative to the PEP concept for investors with no CGT worries. Although you lose the tax relief on the dividend income, that is more than compensated by the discount in the investment trust itself and the flexibility and low cost of these schemes. It also gives you an instant widely spread portfolio.

The Business Expansion Scheme offers tax relief on up to £40,000 each year to investors prepared to put their cash into the shares of certain unquoted companies and keep it there for five years. A 50% taxpayer putting £10,000 into a scheme would get £5,000 back from the Inland Revenue. Investors cannot sell their shares within five years or they lose the tax relief. There is no capital gains tax payable when you do sell. The main appeal is to the wealthy who pay high rates of tax and can afford to tie up their money for a minimum of five years.

The companies are high risk and the government has stopped up various loopholes which allowed lower risk ventures such as property to be offered as a BES investment.

Funds allowing you to invest in a basket of BES companies are also on offer.

Treat BES investment with caution. The tax relief is just a bonus. Ignore it when you are making up your mind whether a company or a fund is a worthwhile investment.

A number of companies whose shares have been offered under the BES scheme have been placed in liquidation.

19. **Shareholder discounts**

Companies often regard small shareholders as a nuisance. Sending an annual report and a dividend cheque to someone owning shares worth £500 costs no less than sending the same documentation to an institution with a holding worth £500,000. Other companies take a less jaundiced view. They know that they can rely on the loyalty of most of their smaller shareholders if an unwelcome takeover bid arrives on their boardroom table. They believe that shareholders should use the company's products and tell others about them. Some of these more farsighted companies offer 'shareholder perks'. More formally known as concessionary discounts, perks offer shareholders either free samples or a reduction on one or more of the company's products.

Perks range from a buffet lunch or a package of groceries for shareholders attending the annual general meeting to free seats at the Centre Court during Wimbledon fortnight or the free loan of an entire train on the 14 mile long Romney, Hythe & Dymchurch miniature railway. Perks are frequent among companies involved in the food and drink, hotels and holiday businesses. Perks are unsurprisingly unknown in bulk chemicals or defence electronics.

Literally the last word in shareholder perks was offered to shareholders in one company as they made their final journey on this earth. Dominion International, a company with interests in financial services and natural resources, gave shareholders with 500 shares or more the sum of £250 in cash towards their own funeral. The money was paid when the shareholder died. This seems an odd choice of perk for any company to offer. Dominion's history over the past fifteen years provides the clue. The company was once

known as Dundee Crematorium. Now the crematoria have been
sold and the perk withdrawn. It gained the company macabre
publicity. During the years when the perk was on offer, it was
claimed less than ten times.

European Ferries, the Townsend Thoresen cross channel shipping group, offered the best known perk of all times. Shareholders
putting a few hundred pounds into the company were given up to
50% off ferry fares to the continent. The concession could be used
as many times as the shareholder wanted and only a few peak season
sailings were outside the scope of the perk. Frequent travellers
bought the shares for the perk, ignoring all other aspects of the
investment. The European Ferries share register became larger and
larger with shareholders buying the minimum necessary for the
concession. Eventually, it all got out of hand. The concessionary tail
was wagging the corporate dog. Under pressure from institutional
shareholders European Ferries changed the rules. It gave shareholders a choice between special shares with few benefits other than
cheap travel and conventional shares with no travel concessions.
European Ferries has since been taken over by P & O but the perk
continues.

Some perks require the purchase of just one share. Others
demand greater expenditure. All England Tennis shares cost over
£10,000 each. They are normally sold in pairs so that your spouse,
friend or business associate can sit next to you. A stockbroker will
happily buy you one or two shares for Wimbledon but would not
take kindly to buying one share in Pavion International which once
offered a free sample of its 'Wet 'n' Wild' lipsticks to all shareholders. The same strictures would apply to buying one share in
William Sinclair Holdings. This garden products group once gave all
shareholders a packet of onion seeds and invited them to compete in
growing the largest shareholder onion. You can have one share if
you insist, but expect to pay commission of at least £10.

You should never buy shares just for the concession even if it
appears to be an amazing bargain. Companies can always withdraw
it or change the entry level. Buy the shares only if you are convinced
of their investment merits. The only exception to this rule is the All
England Debenture whose sole value consists in a supply of
Wimbledon tickets. Other than that, the debentures have a life
limited to five years, bear no interest and holders are only offered
the face value of £500 on expiry – plus priority booking for the next
five years.

Beware the discount that turns out to be a premium. One or two garage groups have offered what appeared to be worthwhile discounts on new cars. The only snag was that anyone walking off the street into the same garage could have got an even bigger discount – just for the asking.

Allied-Lyons offer discounts on wines, hotel weekends, restaurant meals and a trip on Loch Lomond to all shareholders

Asprey offers a 15% discount on a range of luxury goods to holders of 750 shares (worth about £5,000)

BSG International gives a 50% discount on Britax car safety equipment to all shareholders

Barrett Developments offers discounts on new houses for shareholders of one year's standing holding at least 1,000 shares (worth £1,500)

Bellway offers discounts on new houses. The qualification is 1,000 shares (worth about £1,600) and a year on the share register

Burton Group gives three 20% vouchers to all shareholders. The vouchers can be used in any of the group's outlets. A purchase of 300 or more shares allows a 12½% discount at stores in the Debenhams chain

Grand Metropolitan give all shareholders a discount on selected group holidays, discounts on wine, beer and spirits and money off the price of Princess Dumbells and Executive Dumbells (for the female and male bodybuilding shareholder)

Hawtin offers all shareholders discounts on wet suits and concessions on life assurance

Kwik-Fit – holders of 100 shares (worth about £85) receive 10% discount on tyres, exhausts, clutches and suspension parts

Lonrho has a range of discounts including reductions on hotel bills in Acapulco to lower prices on Volkswagen and Audi cars. You need 100 shares (worth about £225) to qualify

Alfred Preedy offers a 10% discount in its stores if you hold at least 250 shares (worth about £350)

Riley Leisure gives all shareholders a 20% discount on billiard and snooker tables

Sketchley offers a 25% discount on all its cleaning and repairing services. You need 300 shares (worth about £1,300)

Whitbread offers all shareholders concessions on wine and beer. There are also special shareholder facilities at sporting events which Whitbread sponsors.

(Source – Seymour Pierce & Co, stockbrokers.)

Full details of shareholder concessions are published once a year by
Seymour Pierce & Co, 10, Old Jewry, London EC2R 8EA at £1.50.
Kleinwort Grieveson, stockbrokers, 59, Gresham Street, London
EC2P 2DS also publish a list.

20. **Taxation**

Whether you invest by a system involving days of roasting your eyes in front of a computer or leave it all to someone else you will face that great inevitable in a buff envelope – taxation. You will need to keep records whether you make or lose money. Eventually, you will have to declare dividend income and realised capital gains and losses on your income tax return.

No one wants to pay more tax than is necessary. Investment packages which offer tax concessions appear attractive. These include pension plans, personal equity plans, the business expansion scheme and insurance bonds. But there is one iron rule covering investment and taxation. You should never make an investment decision – either to buy or to sell – solely on the basis of a tax advantage. Putting £10,000 in a business expansion scheme company and saving save £2,900 in tax at the basic rate is a waste of money if the BES venture flops and you lose the other £7,100. Before putting your money into a 'tax saving investment', ask yourself if you would invest without the presumed tax benefits. If the answer is yes, work out if the tax saving overcomes costs and restrictions on your freedom to sell your investments.

A favourite City story shows how tax considerations can cloud an investor's mind. In late 1969, there was a tiny Australian mining company called Poseidon. The shares were valued at less than a pound. Poseidon was alleged to have huge deposits of nickel, a mineral in demand at the time. The share price started to soar. As often happens in mineral booms, investors then buy the shares of whoever owns land adjoining the target company and then shares of mining companies even further afield are chased.

By the time the crocuses started to come out in 1970, Poseidon shares had soared to £120 and shares in other companies caught up in the madness had increased twenty and forty times. Yet no one in the United Kingdom sold despite increasingly convincing reports that the nearest Poseidon had got to nickel was the plating on the canteen spoons. What caused this paralysis among UK investors? The answer lies in the tax system of the time. This taxed any gains on shares held less than one year at extremely high rates. UK investors held on, Australian and other investors sold. By the time it was safe to sell Poseidon from the taxation viewpoint, the shares were all but worthless.

More recently, the claim of tax advantages was used as the bait to persuade British investors to put their money into some distinctly odd looking property investments in Panama. The sales organisation promoting these property bonds told investors that the very high promised income would be entirely tax free. The Inland Revenue did not agree.

Investors in stocks and shares who live in the United Kingdom face two taxes. The first is income tax, which is levied on the dividend income from shareholdings. The second is capital gains tax which you pay on any profits you make on the value of your shares or unit trusts.

And now for a pleasant surprise. Although Capital Gains Tax (usually abbreviated to CGT) can be horrendously complicated and is currently calculated at 30%, most people never pay a penny – and that is all quite legal. Before you have any liability to pay, you have to realise the gain by selling the shares. And before you actually hand over hard cash to the Inland Revenue, there is the considerable cushion of a tax free allowance. There is no tax payable on paper gains – profits that you could make by selling but choose not to. In any tax year when you do not sell any shares, there can be no CGT worries. Nor are there any worries if your sales are limited to government stocks and company loan stocks which were taken out of the CGT net in July 1986.

At some stage, you will either want or need to sell shares. Assume you sell shares in five companies in one tax year and make a profit on all but one. Add up all the gains and take away the loss. That gives you the chargeable gain. Losses on government stocks or company loan stocks do not count. If the end result is within the tax free slice (£6,300 in the year to April 1987), you are again sitting pretty although you will have to declare the gain. The tax free figure has gone up each year for the past few years. There is of course no guarantee that it will continue to rise but the present limit means that most private investors pay little or no tax. The one drawback to the £6,300 rule is that husband and wife count as one except in their year of marriage – another example of where tax law favours those living in what was once known as sin. A couple living in unmarried harmony could have two free slices.

But the yearly 'free' slice of CGT is not the end of the story. The price you paid for the shares at the time of their purchase is then adjusted for inflation between that time and the time of the sale. Inflation is measured by the government's retail prices index. If you purchased £100,000 of shares in January 1986 and sell those shares for £150,000 in January 1988, the gain will be calculated on £100,000 plus whatever the percentage gain in the retail prices index between the two dates. Assume that is 10%. Your adjusted cost of the shares is now £110,000. The capital gain is now £40,000 from which you can subtract the tax free slice. Had you made a loss – suppose you were forced to sell the shares for £80,000 – indexation will increase your loss. If your losses exceed your gains, the loss can be carried forward to future years. You cannot, however, ask for a cash rebate from the Inland Revenue.

Once you have deducted your losses, your free slice and your indexation from your profits, you have to pay 30% of what is left.

If you sell part of a holding, the calculations are made on the part sold, not on the whole. If you have built up a holding in one share over many years – a monthly investment or unit trust savings scheme would be an example – your holding is 'pooled' and an average purchase price is calculated.

If the company in which you hold shares is subject to a takeover bid, you will be liable for CGT if you accept cash. If you take shares of some sort in the company making the bid, you have no problems until you come to sell those shares.

The costs involved in buying and selling shares are also deductible from a CGT calculation. Keep all contract notes. The contract note is also the only way you can establish what you paid for the shares. It is not printed on the certificate.

You cannot avoid the need to keep CGT records even if your gains are unlikely to exceed the annual free slice. The tax rules might change. A future budget could move CGT to a new method of calculation. There is an endless range of permutations possible and some would be distinctly less friendly than the present method.

The tax can also apply to other profits you make by selling something – the sale of a business or a second home would be examples. If you sold shares at the same time, all your CGT liabilities would be added together but you would still only qualify for one tax free slice. So again, record-keeping is essential.

The second tax associated with the Shares Game is income tax. The bright spot is that most people will pay it without pain. They will not even know they have paid it. Income tax is payable on dividends arising from all the shares, stocks, investment and unit trusts that you own. With a few exceptions, these payments are sent to you with basic rate income tax already deducted. This is known as paying 'net of tax'. In the tax year 1986–87, basic rate income tax was charged at 29% on the first £17,200 of your income. For most people this figure includes the value of benefits in kind such as a company car, subsidised loans or company housing but is calculated after certain deductions such as pension contributions and personal allowances.

Well over 90% of the UK population pays no more than basic rate tax on their income. They pay no additional tax on net dividends. It has been paid on their behalf. However, they must still declare the payment on their tax return. If you are within this category, your tax inspector will gross up the payment – multiply it by 100 and divide it by 71 (100−29) to find out how much you would have received had the tax not been deducted. This could push you into a higher tax band if your income is near the upper limit for basic rate tax or – if you are retired and claiming age allowance – push you into the age allowance trap.

It is not all one way, however. If your income is very low and you pay no tax, you can reclaim the tax paid on your behalf in contrast to bank or building society interest. Children can also reclaim tax unless their annual income (including covenants) is more than the single person's allowance (£2,335 in 1986–87). The one exception is if the money to buy the shares came from the parents. Any other source – grandparents, aunts and uncles, godparents or friends of the family – is fine.

If your income, including grossed up investment income, pushes you into a higher tax bracket, you will have to pay the difference between your highest rate of tax and the basic rate already deducted. If you receive dividends worth £35.50 net and your top tax rate is 50%, the tax inspector will gross up the dividends to £50, charge you at 50% but deduct the £14.50 already paid from the £25 you owe. Your tax bill is £10.50.

Some dividends are paid gross. These include government stocks purchased through the National Savings Stock Register at a Post Office, War Loan (wherever purchased) and certain overseas shares and offshore unit trusts. Tax must be paid on all such dividends unless your income is very low.

When gilts were taken outside the CGT net, other less favourable changes were brought in to stop a tax dodge known as bond washing or dividend stripping. You have now to pay income tax not just on dividends received but also on 'accrued income'. Accrued income is the amount that would be added each day to the value of a gilt if the interest was paid daily. If you have £10,000 of gilts which pay out a 10% gross yield, you would expect £500 gross every six months. If you sell them three months after the last ex-dividend date, it is assumed that you have received accrued income of £250. You will not see this as a separate sum. It is tied up in the price you get and was previously treated as a capital gain. However, if your total nominal holdings of stocks within the accrued income scheme do not exceed £5,000 in the current or previous tax year, you can ignore accrued income. Your gain will be tax free. Securities within the accrued income scheme include government stocks, local authority and company loan stocks and certain special forms of Stock Exchange quoted building society bonds.

Beware of the term 'tax-free'. Other than the first £70 of interest on a National Savings Bank Ordinary Account, Premium Bond prizes and National Savings Certificates, pension funds, charity funds and the personal equity plan, every other form of investment attracts tax in one way or another. Sales literature, especially for insurance bonds and insurance-linked savings schemes are peppered with phrases such as 'tax free' and 'no personal tax liability'. What they mean is that the individual may have no tax to pay but the insurance company certainly will. The payment of the tax may be painless, but it will be paid nonetheless. In some cases, tax free can mean paying more.

This can lead to confusion between unit trust investments which are taxed in the same way as any share investment and insurance bonds. The two often sound the same. Often they are the same shares managed by the same people. The Supagro Ruritanian Emerging Companies Growth Insurance Bond or Savings Scheme is likely to have exactly the same portfolio as the Supagro Ruritanian Emerging Companies Growth Unit Trust and its associated savings scheme. There the similarity ends. The unit trust and the insurance bond are subject to entirely different tax rules and this applies both to the capital gains or losses and income received within the fund and to the eventual capital gain or loss and income received by the owner of the bond or unit trust.

Insurance-based investment products are normally only suitable for higher rate taxpayers and those with enormous capital gains. They may also be suitable for older people caught in the age allowance trap. For anyone paying basic rate tax and whose capital gains are modest, the parallel unit trust is the best bet. The Lloyds Bank Smaller Companies Recovery Unit Trust was set up in February 1980. It has been a good performing unit trust. Over one recent five-year period, it had turned an initial £1,000 investment into £3,670. Black Horse Life is a subsidiary of Lloyds Bank. In February 1980, Black Horse set up a Smaller Companies Recovery Fund whose only investment is in the units of the similarly named trust. Over the same five-year period with exactly the same investments, it turned an initial investment of £1,000 into £3,012.

The difference has nothing to do with Lloyds Bank but is explained by the tax treatment. Investing in the insurance bond would only be to the advantage of a higher rate taxpayer who could offset the slower performance by using the tax rules applying to insurance bonds. A basic rate taxpayer would have lost £658.

INDEX

Management